REVENUE OFFICER

B2B SUCCESS MODEL

Sales Revenue System 2.0

CARL MOE

Sales Revenue System 2.0: Your Chief Revenue Officer B2B Success Model

C.R.O. Success, LLC
1609 W. Cty Rd. 42 #156
Burnsville, MN 55306
www.CROSuccess.com

Third Printing, January 2011

ISBN 978-0-615-30333-8

Edited by Emily Therneau

Design and Layout by BRIO, Minneapolis, MN

Printed in the United States of America

CONTENTS

DEDICATION

When I read a sappy book dedication dragging on and on about the many hours and long days the author(s) devoted to writing the book, it makes me chuckle (and roll my eyes). If they had ever worked in sales, they would already be accustomed to extended work hours.

This book is dedicated to those Chief Revenue Officers who start out every work day with the goal of moving their organization's revenue performance to the next threshold of achievement—from first order to breakeven to exceeding the growth objective for the year. The goal is to make those days more productive by providing a structured Revenue System that is straightforward to understand, adopt and manage.

INTRODUCTION

"PLAIN QUESTION AND PLAIN ANSWER MAKE THE SHORTEST ROAD OUT OF MOST PERPLEXITIES."

MARK TWAIN

We have followed Twain's wisdom in preparing this text. It pushed us to boil our revenue system knowledge down to the essentials. We write this for all the business owners and executives who know they have a viable business offering and want to ensure their revenue performance is not compromised by a nonexistent or misaligned revenue structure.

This handbook is the result of a substantial team effort involving business partners, associates, clients and strategic sales minds from multiple industries that supported the idea of a roadmap guide for Chief Revenue Officer (CRO) success, encouraged its development, and contributed unselfishly to the content. They are the collective "we" in this publication.

What's this revenue thing all about???

The Chief Revenue Officer role is not taught in college; unlike our legal profession, Chief Revenue Officers only pass the "Revenue Bar" on the *street*—this is not a classroom sport. Failing on the street has many consequences ranging from needing a new career to learning the intricacies of our bankruptcy system, all of which are challenging, but seldom rewarding.

> **Chief Revenue Officer (CRO):**
> *noun.* the person or position within any business whose responsibility (aka: butt on the line) it is to make certain revenue is generated to a) stay in business and meet monetary obligations, b) deliver profit, c) grow the company, d) meet and/or exceed financial needs for future growth—also called *rainmaker, President, CEO, COO, Owner, VP of Sales, VP of Business Development or Sales Mgr.*

Revenue production is a common business process few management teams truly understand, that is until they don't have enough revenue. Our goal is to help those dedicated teams get their revenue system implemented and operational before they run out of time. This is the motivation for writing this handbook.

Our target audience is Chief Revenue Officers of start-up to mid-size companies (essentially those companies with little or no revenue to those with not enough revenue) selling both products and services where they are subject to one or more of the following:

- Competing with larger and better funded competitors where sales cycles are more than a "one call close" model
- Campaigns that are expensive to conduct and frequently involve teams of experts to help define/position your products and solutions
- Competitive disruption due to technology innovation and advancements
- Decision processes that cross prospect organizational boundaries (become "geo-political")

We have witnessed enough companies struggling to meet their revenue objectives to realize the 80/20 rule applies to the Chief Revenue Officer function. No matter what the business, eighty percent of the Chief Revenue Officer's role has common, core requirements (coaching, accountability, motivation, and staffing for your revenue system) and the remaining twenty percent is unique to the industry and organizational culture of the company. Recognizing that no two companies—even in the same industry—are identical, we have focused on the heavy lifting demanded by the eighty percent and do not address the culture and style differences that profile the remaining twenty percent of the Chief Revenue Officer role.

WARNING!

There are small-minded management teams out there who hold an all too common view that sales is simply a "glossy brochure delivered by a talking head over an expensive lunch." Unfortunately, this is a common profile and NO revenue system will perform effectively in this culture. Hopefully this describes your primary competition. If you don't put them out of business, their lack of a Revenue IQ will eventually conclude their existence, so start pursuing their customer base today.

We expect you to gain both a new Chief Revenue Officer perspective and a hands-on understanding of the core processes that make up a true Revenue System.

MEET THE AUTHOR

Carl Moe

Carl's career began in Detroit selling computer-based design and production automation systems to the Big 3 auto companies for Digital Equipment Corporation. Next were decades of officer and executive roles in technology-based growth organizations including President, Rank Sherr Tumico, Inc. (US subsidiary of The Rank Organization, Plc); Executive Vice President, Midwest Systems, Inc.; Vice President of Sales & Marketing, CyberOptics, Inc.; and Chief Operating Officer, NT International, Inc. prior to becoming an executive coach and corporate resource for installing Revenue Systems in growth-oriented companies.

Making the numbers is always Carl's top tier objective and to do that more successfully, he created the **Four ♣ Aces** Forecast Model, essentially eliminating blue-sky sales projections based only on "hope and smoke." The process is detailed in this text and is frequently referred to by clients as the "Bankable Forecast."

Carl holds both an engineering degree and MBA from the University of Michigan. When he is not working with clients building revenue systems, he is active with his farming operations. Carl was recognized as Conservationist of the Year by the local Pheasants Forever Chapter in 2008.

SECTION I

The Don't Ask, Don't Tell Sales Model

Chapter 1

CHIEF REVENUE OFFICER

If your primary work responsibility is producing the revenues necessary to keep your board of directors and investors happy (including your sometimes less-than-friendly banker), you are the Chief Revenue Officer (CRO). Your title may be CEO, President, COO, VP of Sales, Business Development Director, etc., but when the company's revenue success (or failure) lies squarely on your shoulders, consider yourself the Chief Revenue Officer. This book has been written specifically for your success, survival, and sanity.

So, why have a sales force?

The only reason to have a sales force
is to alter the prospects' decision process
*so they **value your competitive differentiation***
***more than a lower price**.*

The primary indicator of an ineffective sales force is when you know and your sales team confirms that your product or service brings real value to the marketplace but they still need lower prices to close business. If your sales force is not able to alter the prospect's decision process, then it is time to get a team in place

CRO Success Rule #1:
When all four tires on your car are flat, putting some air in one tire does not remedy the situation. This is why most companies feel sales training doesn't work...and it won't work as long as they ignore the other core processes of a complete Revenue System.

A complete listing of the CRO Success Rules is located on page 124.

that can. Our observation is the sales team either needs training on how to articulate and defend your Differentiating Values or you need a more robust sales force selection process.

With decades of business experience, we've had the opportunity to witness revenue disasters of quantum proportions. Every company we've worked with has expressed some version of the same basic narrative:

- "Our business situation is unique"
- "We've got the best (or worst) sales team in the market"
- "Our market is very competitive"
- "We're getting beat up on price"
- "New prospects always take a serious look at us before they pass"
- "Our quality, service, and support are truly world class"
- "Our sales staff always has a full sales pipeline"
- "We have a very long sales cycle"

One of the most routine phone calls is a version of this message: "We are really hurting for short-term revenue! Can you help us out?"

The answer is always, "Of course we can." There are several effective, short-term measures that can be done to kick-start the revenue flow, but the REAL fix is to help Chief Revenue Officers understand and act on the fact that revenue is a system management issue just like any other well-run production discipline.

Chapter 2

TANKING REVENUE

It's the silent, destructive, and sometimes terminal epidemic that quietly and invisibly invades even the most well-run companies. It can wreak havoc on revenues and profits for years before it's identified and that's if the company is lucky.

This chronic business epidemic is not selective. It can surface in any industry, in large corporations or small businesses. It does *not* discriminate. No company, no matter how profitable, is immune. It operates globally and does not require an internet connection.

The first signs are often ignored, like the empty coffee pot in the company's break room; then it's misdiagnosed. As it sabotages revenue projections and drains profits, the often well-meaning executive team may panic and throw money at it hoping that it will go away. When that doesn't work, executives may follow the sales department's suggestion and cut prices...and profits. This may temporarily give the company a blip on the EKG, but the inevitable flat line will follow.

We're talking about tanking revenue. As Chief Revenue Officer, you understand, perhaps more than anyone else, that your company can't operate on air alone, it needs money! The only sustainable way to generate that money (excluding ongoing government bailouts) is through profitable sales.

At first, the revenue symptoms are barely discernable: sales are a little flat or as sales describes, "It's the slow season." Then margins begin to thin, to remain competitive. This pattern can continue on for a few months to a few years assuming one can afford to let it linger that long.

The board of directors then begins pressuring the management team for more and more sales with improved margins.

Sales contends that they're doing all they can. Their hands are tied. The market has become cyclical and it just happens to be on the downside at present. It's just the pattern.

Sales digs in further and then issues a remarkable turnaround forecast. Significant pieces of business are on the way, yet they need a little edge (i.e., major price concessions) over the competition, which they admit is fierce. Sales confirms that the company's advantage is slight at best and a price reduction would help capture the outstanding business.

Getting pressure from both sides, the executive team feels compelled to act. It's critical to see some check marks in the win column, yet everyone hates to do it by cutting margins. A couple new orders just might ease the board's demands.

It doesn't take a rocket scientist to figure out that cutting margins is a short term cure at best, and it can only be repeated a few times before the company has positioned itself to a near zero profit condition.

There are variations of this revenue trend played out throughout the country, in all industries, and in all markets. It's not unique, yet it IS avoidable.

Discounting Despair – the painful impact

1. Assume an $8,000 order with a gross margin of 30%. The gross margin revenue in this order is:

   $8,000 x 30% = $2,400

2. A 10% discount yields a $7,200 order with a new "discounted" gross margin revenue of:

   $2,400 minus $800 (the 10% discount amount) = $1,600

   $1,600 is 22% of the $7,200 sale = the new "discounted" gross margin percentage

3. The new order volume required at a 10% discounted price to produce the original $2,400 of gross margin is:

   22% x New Revenue = $2,400

   New Revenue = $2,400 / .22 = $10,909 which is 136% of the initial $8,000 order at 10% discounted prices to recover the original $2,400 of gross margin

Graphically expanding our example to other discount levels:

	1	2	3	4	5
■ Target Profit/Margin 30%	$2,400	$2,400	$2,400	$2,400	$2,400
Percentage of Discount	0%	5%	10%	15%	20%
■ Sales Needed to Hit Target Profit	$8,000	$9,230	$10,909	$13,333	$18,462
Percentage of Sales Increase Needed		115%	136%	167%	231%

Obviously, discounting is not a viable long term strategy—especially if you don't have additional market availability to recover your gross margin requirements.

Chapter 3

THE COVER-UP

For anyone who has ever scrambled to make a payroll or meet a critical bank payment, you understand the frustration when all of the company's cash requirements had been "covered" by an earlier sales forecast that didn't materialize. You know what we're talking about. Remember, the sales forecast where the sales group so eloquently explained why things are "slow" today, but "guaranteed" an over-the-top recovery next quarter.

Fast-forward to next quarter, here you sit looking at a sales report with big ZEROS next to the "got 'em in the bag," "sure to close," and "they can't live without us" pieces of business. What happened? How could the sales forecast be so far off? The sales department says it's just a fluke and *next* quarter will make up for this quarter's lower-than-expected numbers. As Chief Revenue Officer, you understand one thing for sure: if this is allowed to continue, the business (and your role) is doomed.

Finger Pointing Begins

Sales

So as the diligent Chief Revenue Officer, you approach your sales manager to get to the bottom of why current projections are so off the mark. Not surprisingly, the sales manager has answers and they undoubtedly take the form of one of the following:

- "All the big decisions seem to be holding off until fall. You know, we've really been noticing a definite market cycle for our products. It's sure to be picking up and the sales team is working hard to make that happen."

- "Yeah, I know we have a lot of proposals pending out there, but they're all hot and ready to close any day. Next month will be huge...maybe the best ever!"

- "Some of the no's were a total surprise to the sales reps. We predicted most of them to close before the end of the quarter, but for different reasons they ALL fell through..."

- "We would have closed XYZ Company, but after they got our proposal, they decided to stay where they are. It appears their current vendor matched our offering."

- "As for 123, Inc., and ANE Company, they both said our prices were too high. You know, we really need to take another look at our mark-up. If we dropped our prices we'd be more competitive and we might still get this business."

- "We really feel good about where we're sitting with ABC and Sons. They said they absolutely love and need what we offer. ABC even confessed that our competitor can't do half the things we can do. However, their hands are tied because they don't have the budget to afford us. Their purchasing agent told us that if we matched the price of their current supplier, we'd have been in yesterday."

- "And, with Acme Corp., they got our proposal at the beginning of the quarter and they are still thinking about it. I'm positive it will close this quarter."

- "We in sales have been discussing how marketing seems

to be bringing us fewer and weaker leads. They need to pick up the pace over there and get in the game."

- "Our sales people have been booked solid with appointments for months. We couldn't get in front of more prospects without hiring more sales people."

- "The number of proposals we're being asked to generate… whew, it's staggering. When all those deals hit, it's going to look like an order Tsunami around here."

As you drill down the list of earlier deals that mysteriously "disappeared" from the latest forecast, the sales manager explains away each and every one:

- "They said our price was too high."
- "We are probably better off—engineering thought it might not work anyway."
- "Our inside contact was at a seminar when they made the decision."
- "The competition must have seen our quote."
- "That one ended up as a committee decision."
- "They decided they wanted a new vendor."
- "They lied about what they really wanted."
- "It was the best looking proposal package we have ever submitted."
- "We gave them ten reference accounts…"
- "We asked for a call back before they made the decision, but we never heard from them."

As Chief Revenue Officer, what can you say? Everything the sales manager says seems plausible. Sales have been sluggish before. Maybe it *is* cyclical. The fact that so many possible deals are hanging means that something's got to hit. We may just need more time and more leads, maybe better leads.

Marketing

Next you speak to marketing. The director presents enough market analysis data to crash your entire computer network while explaining how and why the marketing department's efforts are producing superior results:

- "We've put our company name in front of every purchasing agent in the five-state area."
- "The website has been generating record numbers of leads."
- "Our biggest competitor is really going after us. We see them wherever we advertise…so we doubled the size of our ad budget and hired a new creative agency."
- "We promote all of the benefits of our #1 product, but it's been on the street for a long time and isn't attracting the same attention it once did."
- "Sales isn't pushing the right products. We're out there promoting our top-end line, yet sales keeps selling our discounted line."
- "You know…our web site could use an overhaul."

As you leave that meeting, you scratch your head, not sure which direction to go. Everyone is working hard, doing their jobs. Feedback from the department heads seems reasonable and plausible. All metrics appear to be in alignment, yet the numbers are in the tank. Everyone seems to have an answer, yet as Chief Revenue Officer, you're left holding the bag. How could the "rock solid" sales forecast not produce the expected results? Were the reasons described by the sales and marketing managers an absurd coincidence, or is something off the mark?

If any of these scenarios seem familiar, you're not alone. Our observations have seen this phenomenon repeat itself in *all* businesses. It is NOT a random conspiracy carried out by a handful of really bad sales people.

Chapter 4

THE DON'T ASK, DON'T TELL MODEL

Organizations generally blame the sales force when the numbers are sub-par and then engage in a variety of remedies including recruiting the competition, motivational seminars, free trip incentives, psychological evaluations, hiring industry consultants, etc...all with the goal of quickly finding a new revenue formula for their business. If only it was that easy.

One of the most frequent breakdowns we encounter is when the sales forecast suggests enough volume of business to pacify the Chief Revenue Officer. Simply put, the sales forecast is promising enough that the Chief Revenue Officer doesn't feel the need to audit the forecast pipeline for validation or accountability. This is a classic symptom of the Don't Ask, Don't Tell Sales Model.

Toxic Euphoria

From our decades of observing the inner workings of businesses, we discovered that many, if not most, companies subscribe to some form of a Don't Ask, Don't Tell Sales Model. Basically, sales managers vow not to pursue and pressure the sales force for hard numbers, and sales reps promise not to tell the whole truth about the dubious deals included in their forecast numbers. Essentially, the Chief Revenue Officer accepts the optimistic sales forecast as fact and imparts an *all-systems-are-go euphoria* to the rest of the organization, oblivious to what really lies ahead. This is one of the most toxic practices for Chief Revenue Officer success and survival in play today.

YES…There is a better model.

We knew there had to be a better way to accurately predict and generate revenue. Our divide and conquer approach identified four interrelated core processes that constitute a complete Revenue System. Most companies have portions of one or more of these four core processes in operation today. We refer to these existing revenue models as first tier or 1.0 level revenue systems. Our model provides an actionable road map for moving to the next performance level (Revenue System 2.0) along with our data base of best practices for a more effective implementation.

Chapter 5

THE SALES REVENUE SYSTEM 2.0

When we began probing the reasons for revenue short falls, we quickly discovered a pattern. We came to the realization that in almost every other sector of the business, there were processes in place to make certain the company was on track.

There were accounting processes, quality control processes, manufacturing processes, request for time off processes; you name it, there was a process for it. However, there was a glaring omission of any defined selling processes.

We then discovered that a selling process alone wasn't the magic bullet we had hoped. Sometimes it set sales heading in the right direction, but it still wasn't enough. We further discovered that in addition to the sales process, there were three additional critical processes (forecast, incentive and staffing) that needed to be integrated for higher level revenue performance. We refer to this four process model as the Sales Revenue System 2.0.

The Sales Revenue System 2.0 has four integral core processes:

Our experience indicates that most companies are operating on only one or two of these core processes with predictably disappointing results. Companies are limping along, vulnerable to sluggish growth, slower market reactions, instability against competitors, lower margins, and unreliable sales forecasts to name a few.

The four core processes in the Sales Revenue System 2.0 are:

1. **5 M's Sales Process**

We've seen it hundreds of times: We're asked into a company to fix their ailing sales performance. When we request an outline of their selling process, we are handed a one-page commission plan. Period. End of story. Some companies honestly believe that a commission plan is all they need. It is the "just add water and go to the bank" sales approach. In the absence of a structured sales process, you run the risk of experiencing longer sales cycles, lower margins, revenue shortfalls, and a more stressful job.

The first Chief Revenue Officer task is to define the selling process for the business. Our Revenue System model is based on the 5 M's Sales Process. It can be operational in days to weeks (not months to years) since it is based on your business *today* and *not* on hypothetical models of perfect world scenarios that have minimal applicability to the business.

2. **Bankable Forecast Process**

A forecasting system designed by sales people is inevitably designed to help preserve the salesperson's job. Reps that can't sell know they have to look valuable to keep their payroll number active. The quick fix is to pump up the forecast numbers for short term survival. As Chief Revenue Officer, you cannot waste time learning every rep's unique forecast system and you certainly can't rely on its projections for strategic short-term and, heaven forbid, long-term planning. Once you have *your* selling system defined, you will be able to extract the *objective* data to report and determine accurately where you are in the qualifying/sales process with each revenue opportunity. This objectivity provides the foundation for a Bankable Forecast Process.

3. **Results-Driven Incentive Process**

Most companies have a one-size-fits-all mentality about sales commission or incentive plans. We know if the incentive system isn't structured correctly, companies typically wind up losing their strongest performers.

When a company inadvertently rewards its weaker sales members for only casually maintaining business it would have received anyway, even the good reps are tempted to settle into the role of an overpaid account manager. Additionally, companies with this approach realize no significant growth because they don't recognize the true value of new business in their incentive program. This usually concludes with your best talent departing for more lucrative opportunities, leaving you with overpaid and underperforming account "babysitters." Hopefully, this is what your primary competitors are doing today.

4. **Skills-Based Staffing Process**

Once you have defined your selling process, forecast process, and incentive process metrics, you can now identify the desired skills and characteristics required for your sales positions. By defining and communicating the required skill sets, you will be screening and selecting applicants based on who *can* and *will* sell in your marketplace. The real benefit is eliminating the emotional hiring that produced the crew you have today.

Chapter 6

THE CHIEF REVENUE OFFICER CHALLENGE

There are numerous high-octane business concepts designed to help companies competitively position their products and services through a variety of market-mapping models. Some "business experts" also suggest that once you complete the "market positioning process," you can super-size your sales force, arm them with these new discoveries, and all that remains is to watch the money roll in. Then you wait...wait...wait...wait...and wait. These tactics may have some validity for part of the business, but they do not address the revenue system fundamentals.

If you survive to "gray hair status" as a Chief Revenue Officer (or no hair as the case may be), you eventually realize these maneuvers cannot be confused with sustainable, process-based revenue growth. Here's why:

The best market positioning and product planning doesn't hold water when the first new prospect responds with, "Yeah, yeah, yeah...all I want is a better deal."

If you have a product that requires human interaction to sell (as opposed to airline web sites selling their product through seating-capacity software programs), it's critical to have a process-based revenue system built into your business model to deliver sustainable revenue success—and not be dependent on luck at the revenue roulette wheel.

We want you to realize that we're not talking strictly about sales, but the *system* of revenue management. As Chief Revenue Officer, you need to understand how to manage (i.e., synchronize) the four critical revenue processes with such accuracy that you and the company can unhesitatingly rely on your revenue, margin, and growth projections.

We assume there are other models that work too and if you already have one, stay with it. Our efforts here are geared toward those Chief Revenue Officers who are experiencing more challenge than success (what we refer to as Revenue System 1.0 level performance) and who need to remedy their revenue situation today.

SECTION II

The 5 M's Sales Process

Chapter 7

THE 5 M's

Any sales process, when boiled down to its basic elements, is rather straightforward. Unfortunately, the simple street-tested elements of a sales process are not routinely taught in the business schools we've encountered. Instead, business classes often fill you full of widgets, marketing campaigns, and business schemes that theoretically might work. Let's face it, you're running a business, you don't need a questionable theory, you need reliable systems and processes that work in the real world.

In our decades of selling, leading sales forces, and consulting with revenue teams, we have encountered thousands of different sales scenarios. From a quick glance, they all seemed unique in their own way; however, a clear-cut pattern began to emerge. We came to tag them as the 5 M's:

Message
Motivation
Money
Methodology
Market

When all five of the M's are achieved, you have the foundation for an objective, measurable sales process. However, with each missing M we saw the sales productivity drop somewhere between circling the wagons (revenues are flat) to circling the drain (revenues are in a downward spiral).

As dramatic as the decline in revenue was to us, we were even more surprised by the percentage of leaders that thought their current process, or lack thereof, was acceptable enough to keep betting on (funding) the future of the company.

In the following chapters, we outline each of the 5 M's and their function in prospect qualifying. Each chapter contains a core set of Critical Qualifying Questions (CQQs) that the sales person uses to start the qualifying dialog for each M element of the sales process.

To better demonstrate how the Critical Qualifying Questions work within the 5 M's Sales Process, we have included examples that we use in our business. We opted out of the generic example approach since most Chief Revenue Officers are already working long days and typically don't have time to translate "generic" into their world. Seeing these tools in use in our world is a hands-on example of how it all works and provides a roadmap of how it can be done in your business.

Chapter 8

MESSAGE

The first M we'll discuss is Message. The message(s) you communicate to prospects that differentiate you from the competition can often mean the difference between selling with a profit vs. having to match the low ball price of your most desperate competitor.

To give you an example, a president of a community bank was asked the question, "How's business?" His response was that they were being beaten down by internet banking and no-frills banks. When asked, "What makes your bank different from the rest of the banks?" he paused, and then eloquently said, "We're a community bank with great customer service." It was hard to keep from laughing out loud. What he stated is currently the tagline of almost every community bank across America. Great "quality, service, and support" are generic statements made by *every* business today.

No wonder his margins were tanking. With a bank on every corner, and the lack of a strong message *differentiating* his bank from the competition, the customers had nothing but interest rates to use for comparison. As far as the prospect is concerned, a bank is a bank is a bank.

CRO Success Rule #2:
If you're not clear about what makes you worth more, you **will always** compete on price.

A complete listing of the CRO Success Rules is located on page 124.

Is this happening in your company?

Has your company clearly identified what makes you better than the competition—in the minds of the customer, that is? If you are honestly offering more than your competitor and what you offer brings more value to the customer, then you should be worth more, right?

Unfortunately, in today's market you have to *clearly* express what sets you apart from your competitors and your prospects must find this valuable. We're not talking about the traditional features and benefit statements boringly presented on glossy four-color data sheets.

Part of our work with clients includes doing lost sale autopsies… yes, actually dissecting why they lost a sale. Two prospect profiles consistently surface in these activities:

1. Prospects do not invest the time required to fully understand all of your products or service "brilliance," and even if they try, they frequently map your promoted feature/benefit data points into their world incorrectly. This is one reason why feature/benefit-based sales training does not deliver consistent results. It also explains why companies who use this sales approach have longer sales cycles.

2. Prospects make better decisions when you translate your unique product or service capabilities into their world for them. After all, that is where they live, work and make decisions.

CRO Success Rule #3:
If a prospect decides not to do business with your company and there is no impact in his/her world as a result of that decision, the person made a good business decision. As such, your Message objective is to make sure prospects understand what they will give up (lose) if they decide not to do business with you.

A complete listing of the CRO Success Rules is located on page 124.

So you face two challenges:

1. Bridge the communication gap between you and the prospect's world.

2. Do it in a way that will help shorten the overall sales cycle (defined as getting the prospect decision sooner rather than later).

To address these challenges, the Message is based on defining your Differentiating Value. Differentiating Value is what you do that is unique or better than the competition and it is what prospects give up (lose) when they decide not to do business with your company.

Client Example

One of our clients moped into our office and announced that he had just lost his biggest customer who had been with him for ten years. The product was cinnamon used in commercial food processing applications. The customer went to another supplier whose price was three cents per pound lower. He wanted to know how he could win the customer back.

We started the dialog by asking him to answer this question:

"What's going to happen to your clients if they are *not* buying cinnamon from you, and how will that impact *their* lives?"

As we worked through the answer, here is how the story unfolded:

A new purchasing agent called our client and said, "I understand you've been providing us with great service, and we've never had a problem with you in the ten years we've been doing business. However, I noticed you charge us three cents a pound *more* for your cinnamon than I can get it from any of your competitors. Out of respect for the ten-year relationship, I want to give you the chance to match that lower price before I move the business."

At this point the rep started explaining core competencies like quality, service, and support, and the fact that he sold them the cinnamon in smaller batches. This meant the customer didn't have to buy and inventory a large quantity of cinnamon, running the risk of it not being fresh enough when they used it. The buyer kept coming back to the three cents per pound price difference and eventually the business was lost.

Our client had substantial Differentiating Value, yet he was not articulating the message in terms related to the client's world. So now he was being forced to compete on price rather than the myriad of other deliverables he brought to the table.

We asked again, "***What is going to happen to your clients if they are no longer buying cinnamon from you, and how will that impact their lives?"***

After some thought, the rep said it would take them approximately three weeks longer to bring a product to market.

We then asked, "What does a three week delay to market mean in their world?"

The rep said, "You see, the customer is a generic food products manufacturer. When a new food product is introduced by a leading consumer goods producer, this company manufactures a generic version comparable to and competitive with the branded product. The generic food manufacturer wants to get it to market as quickly as possible because food distributors want a generic product that sells at a lower price with higher margins.

The food distributors and the generic food manufacturer want to capitalize on the marketing hype created by the branded product. Time to market is everything in this case. Because the generic product offers higher margins, grocers put a little flag on the shelf that says, "Generic product available at the end of the aisle."

Next we asked the rep, "Why will it take the manufacturer three weeks longer to get their product to market if you don't supply the cinnamon?"

Well, apparently the rep is an expert with regard to the application of spices and preservatives to food products. He nearly has a PhD in the area of food science. He said, "In exchange for them buying the cinnamon from me and paying me a slight premium over the years, I have shared my expertise in food science, spices, and preservatives with their technical department, enabling them to quickly copy the characteristics of the branded product. Without my involvement, they have estimated it will take the technology department at least three weeks longer to get any product to market."

We then asked what three weeks meant in monetary terms and the rep explained that once they get a new product successfully up and running, one day's sales revenue is typically eighty thousand dollars. Three additional weeks translates to $1.6 million in lost revenue opportunities. He also said they launch approximately six products a year at this level.

Excited at this revelation, we asked him, "Do you understand what you've just told us?"

And he said, "Not really."

"Okay, here's what's going to happen: The purchasing agent is going to go to the company's annual banquet and get a plaque for saving the company about $1,200 on the forty thousand pounds of cinnamon he contracted at the lower price. But, there's someone else who will not be able to go to the annual banquet because they will be in a meeting with senior management explaining a $10 million "time to market" revenue shortfall and/or market share loss! Who is the person explaining that loss to senior management?"

The rep said, "That would be the chief marketing executive or the brand manager for that product line."

So, "Who's your real customer?"

He said, "Now that I think about it, it's the brand manager."

"Do you know that person's name?"

He looked rather sheepish and said, "No, I've never talked to that person."

We instructed him, "Let's talk about what you're going to say when you contact the brand manager. We know for sure that he or she **will not** talk to you if the word "cinnamon" crosses your lips. **The message must be about the *consequences of not having your support* because they are not buying the cinnamon from you."**

CRO Success Rule #4:
For a shorter sell cycle, your Differentiating Value message(s) should be directed toward the emotional decision maker, describing what he/she will *lose* without you.

A complete listing of the CRO Success Rules is located on page 124.

Our client was pulling a classic salesperson's mistake by allowing the customer to focus on price instead of the value being delivered to them. Not to mention that his *real* buyer was not the purchasing agent, it was the brand manager. The purchasing agent is who we describe as the **technical buyer**. Technical buyers are *easy to find, hard to close, and most often seeking the lowest price*.

The brand manager however, is the **emotional decision maker**. The emotional decision maker can be described as *the one who suffers the consequences of life without you*. Tell this brand manager it's going to take three weeks longer to market on a new product launch, and you'll hear an immediate response all right. Emotional decision makers are usually harder to find, easier to close, not as price sensitive, and can typically tell the technical buyer what to do.

As the Chief Revenue Officer, you must make certain that clear messages defining how you're different, better, and worth more are used everywhere—sales campaigns, marketing materials, web, etc., and insure that everyone in your company knows and understands why you're better. With your Differentiating Value messages in place, identifying your emotional buyer will be much easier.

Defining your Differentiating Value Messages

1. Define **what matters to the customer** – There is no point in highlighting benefits a customer doesn't care about. View yourself from the prospect's world: As the customer, what do I really care about?

2. **Be unique or demonstrably better** – If the competition offers the same item, whatever that feature/service/product is, then that item is *not* your competitive advantage. In most every industry today, quality, service, and customer support are ALWAYS claimed, so don't even bother to list these unless you can prove you stand alone with *over the top* quality, service and/or support deliverables. Look to other areas where you're better—guarantees, processes, delivery, production savings, time savings, knowledge, exclusives, etc.

3. **Be specific and measurable** – Get rid of the fluff. If you can't be specific and/or measurable, you sound like every other competitor. Don't just claim to be higher quality, offer greater support, or be better overall; prospects have already heard that. What does that mean anyway? How much better? Give prospects relevant justification in their world to prefer your brand and price.

A strong Differentiating Value message is a critical element in the sales process if you intend to get paid what you are worth.

The Differentiating Value questions you need to address are:

- What value do you bring to your customers? (We're talking *real* value here. No fluff.)
- How does the absence of your value show up in the prospect's world?
- Where does it show up?
- Who does it affect?

CRO Success Rule #5:
The breadth and depth of your Differentiating Value platform determines the amount of traction your product or service has in target market segments. It also determines the level of premium pricing you can achieve. **If you have zero Differentiating Value, it means you are selling only on price.**

A complete listing of the CRO Success Rules is located on page 124.

Our 5 M's Selling Process is designed around your Differentiating Value and enables prospects to readily determine the value you bring to their world. The techniques developed in the following sections demonstrate how to use your Differentiating Value to engage the two primary objectives listed earlier:

1. Bridge the communication gap with the prospect's world.

2. Do it in a way that will help shorten the overall sales cycle (defined as getting the prospect's decision sooner rather than later).

Chapter 9

MOTIVATION

The next of the 5 M's is **Motivation**. And we're not talking about the motivation of your salespeople; we're talking about the **motivation of your prospects**. This is the first qualifying step in our 5 M's Sales Process. **If you cannot establish some traction with your Differentiating Value in the prospect's world, you don't have a prospect.**

Face reality: prospects think they are doing fine without you. From the view in their world, everything is good. Prospects don't really care about what you offer because as far as they are concerned, IT DOESN'T AFFECT THEM.

However, instead of just straight out telling your salesperson, "NO," prospects waffle, avoiding concrete answers, feeding your salespeople excuses just to keep them at bay only to have your salespeople coming back for more. All the while, your company continues to spend truckloads of money trying to engage and sway these so-called "hot" prospects. It should be obvious that this is not a good sales process. Yet why is this ineffective practice so prevalent?

After listening to countless stories from sales managers and sales reps explaining why their sales were flat or tanking, it became apparent that at the core, the delays or stalls given by the prospect all had the same DNA. The prospect doesn't see *any* need for what you offer. End of story.

A typical stall sounds like this:

- "I am happy with my current supplier."
- "Our pipeline is covered for now but you are welcome to stop by next quarter if you are in the area."
- "You are not an approved vendor"
- "There may be some room for you but only if your price is substantially better."

Literally, there are thousands of stalls prospects use, yet they all are some variation of the same theme: *I'm doing fine without you, so don't bother me.* Basically, don't count this egg; it won't hatch.

The prospect becomes less passive if, and only if, the consequences of life without you are **exposed and potentially unbearable**. Yet, if the consequences of life without you truly have no adverse effects, then you don't have a prospect.

Client Example

The Chief Revenue Officer of a fastener manufacturing company complained they were experiencing cut-throat price competition in their larger volume manufacturing accounts. He said this was due to customer purchasing department views that any fastener is good enough, so always go for the cheapest bid. This fastener company was not only a quality manufacturing organization (ISO Certifications, Six Sigma quality platforms, etc.); it had world class design engineers skilled at simplifying fastener applications. These design simplifications typically ended up requiring fewer fasteners, and in many cases their engineers were able to help redesign the application and reduce the total number of parts and subassemblies required. These design engineering resources were not available from hardware store type distributors offering the lowest fastener prices.

The short term remedy was to schedule director level meetings with their customers' engineering departments to explain how they could only offer more competitive prices by eliminating their design support. The engineering managers quickly determined that was an unacceptable option and directed their purchasing departments to sole source the designated fasteners from our client. Our client's sales team now understood their Differentiating Value and immediately changed how they introduced and positioned their business to new prospects, thereby eliminating the hardware store distributor option at the start of the sales cycle.

Usually the consequences of life without your product or service aren't horrible, they are just unknown. Therefore, when you can translate the consequences of not being your customer into your prospects' worlds they can start envisioning their own perceptions of new possibilities. The more their perceptions become compelling, the more traction your Differentiating Value has in their decision process.

The fastener manufacturing company actually delivered better product designs to their clients. Obviously their clients could have eventually developed similar designs, but the costs of both additional time and ongoing manufacturing design revisions outweighed the perceived savings of lowest price fasteners.

In the cinnamon sales story the consequences of not having our sales rep's cinnamon, when left in the hands of purchasing (the technical buyer), ended up being a price only decision. As far as the technical buyer was concerned, cinnamon was cinnamon, and it was a commodity. Under further scrutiny, however, the real consequence was a delay in bringing new products to market and the associated revenue loss caused by that delay. To the right person in the organization, in this case the product manager, there was an enormous consequence to not doing business with our sales rep.

Any time your product or service is truly a pure commodity (no real Differentiating Value), your best chance of getting the deal is by offering the lowest price. Of course, our cinnamon sales rep was not selling a commodity (cinnamon), in reality he was selling reduced time-to-market. He merely got paid in cinnamon transactions.

The Flat World Stall

Getting prospects to envision how much better their business can be requires more skill than sending out a promotional e-blast or company brochures with a business card attached. Sometimes what you are telling them *is possible* is so far from what they believe is possible they simply can't believe you. We refer to this as the Flat World Stall.

The Flat World Stall came about at the same time as Christopher Columbus. Columbus was seeking funding for his venture to the New World. Of course, he was being told by all his funding sources that as far as they could tell, the world was flat and they would lose all of their investment when Columbus sailed off the edge.

Essentially, Columbus was being given the first Flat World Stall. From the funding source's view of reality, the world was flat. To bet against this strongly held belief would be nonsense.

Columbus was stymied until he uncovered an effective response: THE WORLD IS NOT FLAT. And because the world is not flat, we can now achieve what had been previously considered unattainable.

What does the Flat World Stall mean to you?

The point of the story is that every stall you get is some variation of the prospect's view of the world, which is flat. And, until you can show your prospects a *new reality* and properly explain it, they'll continue believing they don't need you. Once they understand and accept the possibility of a new reality, such as the world is round, they'll finally be able to envision the new possibilities and the newly revealed consequences.

Your first Differentiating Value based sales objective is to establish your unique product or service value platform with the prospect.

CRO Success Rule #6:
A prospect can never have too much Motivation regarding your Differentiating Value

A complete listing of the CRO Success Rules is located on page 124.

The prospect must understand and see the new options, possibilities, and consequences your Differentiating Value addresses. As stated previously, if the consequences of not doing business with you truly don't affect your prospects, then they are not prospects. However, if they align with wanting/needing your Differentiating Value, you have a prospect and the sales cycle has now officially started.

OUR BUSINESS EXAMPLE

(Reference Differentiating Value questions from page 42)

1. What Value Do You Bring to Your Customers?

We enable Chief Revenue Officers to **consistently** predict, produce, and grow revenue. There is no magic bullet here; it is done through an integrated framework of four core processes that construct a complete Revenue System.

2. How does the absence of your value affect the prospect's world?

A missing or incomplete revenue system increases the frequency of revenue shortfalls, missed forecasts, discounting (reduced margins) and longer, more costly sales campaigns being used to close needed business.

3. Where does your value show up in the prospects' world?

The five primary performance areas impacted by our Revenue System in the Chief Revenue Officer's world are:

- **Revenue Growth**

  Double digit growth is typical for most companies.

- **Margin Growth**

  Typically five to ten percent margin increases are achieved just by eliminating the need to match prices of more desperate/less capable competitors.

- **Forecast Accuracy**

  The forecast goal is plus/minus five percent of the actual number.

- **Shorter Sell Cycles**

  Typical sales cycle reductions are in the twenty percent plus range by simply:

  - eliminating wasted steps in the sales process
  - obtaining the decision earlier so precious sales time is spent on REAL prospects
  - helping qualified prospects make decisions more quickly

- **Talent Selection & Retention**

  Selecting and keeping top-performers is the goal. Losing non-performers is actually a net gain, so not all turnover is bad. Clients routinely upgrade their current sales force within the first year because Chief Revenue Officers are now able to clearly separate poor sales performance from fluctuations in their market and replace marginal performers with better talent in 30 days.

4. Who does it affect first/most?

Initially the Chief Revenue Officer, but ultimately the entire organization.

OUR BUSINESS EXAMPLE

Critical Qualifying Questions (CQQs) regarding Motivation

To uncover if there is any traction between what we offer and what our Chief Revenue Officer prospect is currently experiencing in their world today, we begin by asking questions, not just any questions, but questions focused on our Differentiating Values. These Critical Qualifying Questions (CQQs) are designed to uncover the problems, frustrations, gaps, losses, challenges, etc., that the Chief Revenue Officer is experiencing without us.

Revenue Growth

- What is your sales process today...and what's not working?
- What is the current performance-to-plan gap?
- What is the mix of new vs. existing account business today?
- What is your market share today?
- What growth initiatives have you tried and how are they working?
- How much time do you have left to close the gap?
- What percent of your sales team will exceed goal this year?

Margin Growth

- What percent of current orders are at full price?
- How much longer can discounting be a closing strategy?
- Who initiates discount requests, the sales rep or the prospect?
- Who approves discount offers?
- Do reps earn the same commission for both full price and discounted orders?

Forecast Accuracy

- What is your current forecast process and how is it working?
- Typically, when do you know you are not going to make the forecast?
- How many deals appear to be "welded" to the forecast and never close?
- What is your current forecast accuracy?
- What excuses do you typically hear when reps explain why they are missing their numbers?
- What have you tried so far to improve forecast accuracy?

Shorter Sell Cycles

- What is your typical sales cycle today?
- What keeps you from reducing it—selling skills, selling too low in the prospect organization, etc.?
- Are quotes/proposals typically done first or last in the sales cycle?
- How do you identify the "real" prospects?

Talent Selection & Retention

- What is your turnover rate today and what is that costing you?
- What percent of your sales team will exceed goal this year?
- What is the profile of your best salesperson?
- How long does it take for a new hire to ramp up to full quota?
- How does your incentive plan work?
- How does your on-boarding process work?
- What is your biggest obstacle in finding sales talent today?
- What percent of your current sales team is really in the game vs. just playing the game?

Note: The Critical Qualifying Question process is designed to initiate communication with the prospect in the prospect's world and become the starting point for a focused, qualifying dialog to determine the potential fit your Differentiating Values have with prospects' needs, desires and objectives. If your salesperson works through your Critical Qualifying Questions regarding **motivation** and uncovers that the prospect doesn't have enough traction with your Differentiating Value to make a change to your product or service, then your salesperson has discovered this IS NOT a prospect. At that point it's time for your salesperson to move on and NOT enter this contact on the sales forecast.

Chapter 10

MONEY

Now for the M that gets everyone uncomfortable: **Money**. Having the money conversation with prospects is like playing tug-of-war. The prospect is pulling for the lowest possible cost while the salesperson is tugging for the highest possible price. Often the struggle ends with one of the parties not as excited about the outcome as the other.

What if, in this money tug-of-war, your prospect actually dropped his/her end of the rope? This CAN happen and we've seen it occur repeatedly.

It all goes back to your prospect's mindset. If you've developed and delivered a **strong Differentiating Value message** to the **emotional decision maker** with **compelling consequences** for his/her business without you, your prospect will have less objection to what you cost. You have effectively minimized or eliminated the prospect's resistance because he/she agrees with and understands the consequences of the decision.

Money Is No Object

A few years ago a business partner awoke at 2:00 in the morning

unable to breathe. This is a situation that will get one's attention immediately. As he frantically raced around the house, he realized he could breathe in, but he couldn't breathe out. He was doing everything humanly possible to correct his condition, which of course roused his wife and eventually everyone in the house.
The only thing he could come up with was to give himself the Heimlich maneuver by dropping onto a piano bench and allowing his chest to be struck on its edge. As he struggled to exhale, he became unconscious.

He was awakened later by the medical technicians treating him in the living room. They gave him some relief, put him in the ambulance and transported him to the emergency room of the nearest community hospital, just seven minutes away. Over the next few hours he was able to resume normal breathing.

The most stunning thing of all was the cost of a seven-minute ambulance ride. It was over $1,000 for an uncomfortable, bumpy ride to the local hospital.

As expensive as the brief ambulance ride ended up being, it was during the time period he couldn't breathe, and he wasn't in a position to send out for bids. He needed someone who could respond NOW, and he was willing to pay ANY PRICE. The consequences of not taking the ambulance ride were far greater than a financial hit to his checkbook.

When you can get your salespeople to help their prospects discover that they are in dire need of your product or service, the prospects will take the necessary action to get it and price will not be a problem.

As Chief Revenue Officer, you need to hold sales people accountable for two main qualifying topics related to Money:

1. What are the monetary costs the prospect is experiencing, past, present, and future because he/she is not your customer today and doesn't have your Differentiating Value?

2. How much does the prospect expect to invest to remedy the problems, opportunities, challenges, etc., that your Differentiating Value addresses? If what the prospect intends to spend isn't enough, the job of the sales person is to get more money by reinforcing the consequences and associated costs of not having your Differentiating Value.

When you can get your prospects to realize that the consequences without you could be devastating, the primary decision is no longer focused on your price.

OUR BUSINESS EXAMPLE

Critical Qualifying Questions (CQQ's) Regarding Money

- What does failing to make the revenue number cost the business today?
- What are the margin trends on incoming orders?
- What does it cost the business when you make a bad decision based on an inaccurate sales forecast?
- How long can the business afford to delay a solution?
- What's the budget to fix it?
- What have you considered/tried so far?
- How many lost orders occurred in the last ninety days and what was the total dollar amount?
- What does a below quota sales rep cost per year and how many do you have today?
- If you terminated the two worst performing sales reps, what funding does that open up for a recovery program?

Chapter 11

METHODOLOGY

The next of the 5 M's is **Methodology**. At the time this book was being written, the Minnesota Twins, a professional baseball team, were in their final season playing in an enclosed stadium called The Metrodome. One thing that is interesting about The Metrodome is that there are ground rules unique to that venue.

For example, if a ball is hit into the roof structure and becomes lodged there, it is an automatic double for the batter. If you were playing there, this would be a good thing to know. That's just one of the unique rules to this ball field. The point is what kind of competitive disadvantage would a traveling team have if they came to The Metrodome and did not know the rules unique to that venue?

Baseball recognizes that not knowing the ballpark's quirks would be unfair so there is a meeting at home plate prior to the start of every game where the ground rules are explained to representatives of both teams. The methodology of how a company makes decisions should work exactly the same with regard to the sales process.

Every organization has a method for making decisions. If you don't know their methodology, priorities, and the relative weight of those priorities, you are attempting to play a game where you don't know the rules. This will always cause an ugly, frustrating outcome.

The Chief Revenue Officer's job is to ensure that the sales rep can describe the decision process their prospect will use to evaluate an offer from your firm and decide whether or not to accept that offer. This information is available if the salespeople ask for it. Also, it is essential to understand where you will gain decision points for your Differentiating Value. When your people understand the rules of the game, you greatly increase the likelihood of a win.

OUR BUSINESS EXAMPLE

Critical Qualifying Questions (CQQ's) regarding Methodology

- How does your organization select/utilize outside resources?
- Who is involved in the selection process?
- Who carries the most weight in the final decision?
- Is this a price only decision?
- When was the last time you did not select the low bidder?
- What do you see as the trade-offs between an integrated revenue system solution compared to a piecemeal approach with or without using outside resources?

Chapter 12

MARKET

The final M is **Market**. In business-to-business selling, every deal has competition today. With the globalization of our economy, the number of times we see companies competing with the same traditional list of vendors is disappearing; the days of competing with only one or two primary competitors are over. The internet, 24/7 e-marketing, and search engines literally serve up a world of options for virtually every decision, and more are coming every day. As an example, the last time we searched Google for "sales training" the result was 12.7 *million* listings!

Bringing up the **Market** topic during the sales campaign is almost as uncomfortable as the **Money** discussion. However, the reality is prospects have so many options today that you need to keep the topic on the table during the entire campaign.

The key to eliminating the world of competition is based on how well your Differentiating Value fits with the prospect's desires and objectives. If another solution is potentially a better fit, you want to know that as soon as possible. As Chief Revenue Officer, you then have to make the choice between continuing to pursue the sale with a new strategy or move on to other opportunities. What you don't want to do is stay in the campaign thinking you are still "in play" when you were eliminated weeks or months earlier.

OUR BUSINESS EXAMPLE

Critical Qualifying Questions (CQQ's) regarding Market:

- What other options are you considering?
- Which ones are new to your business and how did you learn about them?
- Which ones do you like so far?
- What are others offering that appeals most to your organization?
- Who have you used in the past and how did that work out?
- What can we speak about today to help you make a decision regarding our integrated Revenue System?

Chapter 13

IMPLEMENTING THE 5 M's SALES PROCESS

Management is responsible for defining their product or service Differentiating Value(s) and the required Critical Qualifying Questions for:

- Motivation
- Money
- Methodology
- Market

Once these are completed, sales reps have a structured qualifying process to follow and a more objective assessment of where they are in terms of completing a sale. This clarity is not only helpful to the rep, it also becomes the foundation for the next core process: The Bankable Forecast.

5 M's Sales Process Installation Work Flow

1. Define your Differentiating Value per the process questions on page 42.
2. For each Differentiating Value listed above, develop your Critical Qualifying Questions (CQQs) regarding Motivation, Money, Methodology and Market.
3. Train your sales teams on this structured qualifying process.
4. Add the process outline into all sales position job descriptions.
5. Schedule ongoing skill development sessions with your sales teams to incorporate and document their updates and enhancements to the process.

What are the early indicators that the process is working?

1. Some accounts drop off the forecast as reps identify the "virtual" opportunities in their pipelines. These discoveries and related disappointments can also cause some rep level turnover.

2. Less sales time is spent reworking quotes, proposals, and presentations.

3. Shorter sales cycles emerge with fewer surprises.

4. Discounting is no longer a closing strategy.

5. Reps have more time available to pursue new business opportunities.

SECTION III

Bankable Forecast Process

Chapter 14

ZERO VISIBILITY SALES FORECAST

The next core process of our Revenue System is the Bankable Forecast. Nothing has deflated the hopes of Chief Revenue Officers more than a sales forecast that reads like fiction. Unfortunately, you often don't know what's real and what's fantasy until the end of the quarter when a string of zeros align next to your salespeople's most promising prospects. However, a reprieve arrives when you are enthusiastically reassured by your sales team that all of the outstanding business is still alive (technically meaning it is not lost... yet) and sure to close sometime this millennium.

When you take a close look at how companies utilize their sales staffs, there are two clear reasons for Zero Visibility Sales Forecasts:

1. Salespeople are allowed to create their own forecast process
2. The forecast process aligns perfectly with the Don't Ask, Don't Tell Sales Model

Left to their own devices, sales reps will routinely forecast optimistic numbers for business that will most likely never close. This spells revenue roulette for the Chief Revenue Officer.

You may have sales people who believe that telling you what you want to hear and keeping their job is better than giving you the truth and risking the possibility of having to seek other employment opportunities. These same reps can effectively convince, in Academy Award winning-style, the sales manager and Chief Revenue Officer that they are doing everything possible to bring in their pipeline. The acting scores a ten, but the revenue is still zero.

Having a flawed sales forecast can produce some sobering consequences:

Missed revenue and margin targets
Maybe you've been surviving okay, meaning the business has been able to turn some profit. But what if a small profit could have been turned into something more substantial? How many real opportunities were missed? Was money left on the table? How many times can you afford to do that? And what if the entire market goes south? When will your current forecast process signal that change?

Mile-high selling costs
A flawed sales forecast can mask poor sales performance and a string of bad prospects for a long period of time. Without a way to accurately identify real business from virtual business, you're wasting time and money on ineffective salespeople and/or the wrong prospects.

Can't get or maintain adequate funding
This is why your forecast process is so important. When your financing resources no longer believe your projections, you are one step closer to becoming an all cash business unless you can get friends and family with enough net worth to co-sign the guarantees.

Symptoms of a flawed forecast:

- High probability prospects never close.
  Instead, projected close dates just keep drifting.

- End of the quarter bulges.
  Does order production come by way of cave-in pricing to meet quarterly budget goals?

- Sales is asking for discounts late in the sales cycle.
  This usually happens because the salesperson skipped a step or two in the sales process, or the prospect wasn't fully qualified.

- No sales forecast definitions.
  You asked your salesperson how he/she arrived at a ninety percent close forecast on a particular prospect and the response was: They are asking a lot of good questions, so they must be really interested!

- Too many high-percentage deals in the forecast.
  Sales may be listing hopeful prospects as "real deals" for their "keep my job" forecast.

- No forecast audit possible
  Each salesperson is allowed to create and use his/her own forecast system.

A Real World Forecast Example

My first Chief Revenue Officer role involved three field sales reps covering the U.S. selling custom engineered power train components. Everything was custom bid with repeat orders being the real goal, assuming the power train product was successful.

As we did the usual monthly forecast submission, I noticed one rep used only two probability numbers for every deal: ten percent or ninety percent. This individual was a twenty-year sales veteran in the industry and I was curious as to how he arrived at those percentages. His answer was, “I put prospects at ten percent if I have some rapport with the receptionist (she gives me the names of the people I need to see) and ninety percent if I can get past the lobby and into the engineering department.”

Needless to say, his entire forecast was at the ninety percent level but he had no closeable business. Any data demonstrating how and why the prospects might want to use our products and services was totally absent. As you might expect, he resigned shortly after the new forecast process was introduced

A Chief Revenue Officer’s survival (and sanity) cannot be based on learning every rep’s sales approach and their related forecast model. The forecast process must have a direct audit trail connection back to the selling process. This connection provides accountability for both your selling process and the resulting forecast data. Keep in mind that flawed sales forecasts are only a symptom of a bigger problem and that’s the lack of overall process accountably.

Chapter 15

CREATING BANKABLE SALES FORECASTS

How many hours do you spend preoccupied, wondering if financial goals and obligations are going to be met? From our experience, most businesses are functioning, albeit below their full capability, with a false set of forecast numbers.

What if your company had a Bankable Sales Forecast? What would that mean for your business?

- Targeting your resources on the real deals – ones where you get paid for your Differentiating Value.
- Achievable (financeable) growth models for the business.
- No cash flow surprises.
- Shortened sales cycles.
- Ability to quickly determine if your salespeople are doing their job.

Our Bankable Forecast Process is based on the four qualifying elements in the 5 M's Sales Process: Motivation, Money, Methodology and Market. Our clients refer to these qualifying elements as the **Four ♣ Aces**. They don't want to keep gambling (investing) more time and money on sales campaigns where they have zero Aces (meaning no traction or fit) with what a prospect wants, needs, or can afford.

Note: We are not promoting gambling with our **Four ♣ Aces** model, but there are at least three similarities between poker and selling that are easily recognized:
First, there are no guaranteed outcomes—everything invested is at risk. Second, there is only one winner. Third, when you draw a bad hand in poker, the wise decision is to minimize your loss and fold. The same applies in sales, but if your sales reps don't know the reality of your position in the deal, they will always push to keep you in the game.

Our **Four ♣ Aces** model is designed to help Chief Revenue Officers identify and **objectively eliminate** second-place-finish campaigns before it is too late and too costly.

Chapter 16

THE FOUR ♣ ACES

The qualifying process definitions of the Four ♣ Aces are:

♥ Ace 1

Motivation Fit is two-fold and means the sales rep has confirmed

1) one or more Differentiating Values are important to the prospect.
2) the prospect is motivated to select and use your products or services because he/she sees your offerings as more advantageous to their business.

♠Ace 2

The Money Discussion has taken place and the prospect

1) understands the monetary consequences of not having your Differentiating Value.
2) fully understands the price he/she has to pay.
3) has the means and desire to pay for your Differentiating Value.

♦Ace 3

Methodology means your sales person fully understands how the decision is being made and knows:

1) how your Differentiating Value is positioned in the decision

process.
2) when the decision is being made.
3) who's making the decision.
4) who breaks a tie.

♣Ace 4

Market Options Eliminated means that all options (including doing nothing) have been

1) identified and discussed with the prospect.
2) the prospect has eliminated them based on needing your Differentiating Value platform..

Now, if you're thinking you can run to the copy machine, hand out this section of the book to your salespeople, and begin receiving Bankable Forecasts, you are wrong. First you need to provide the defined, measured elements for each Ace before it can be "claimed" on a forecast spreadsheet. Just like a doctor prescribes medication, it's also critical that the doctor prescribe the correct dosage in order to obtain the desired results. Patients aren't left to guess how much to take, when to take, and for how long, and neither should your sales force be allowed to determine what enters the sales funnel and how it's rated on the sales forecast. The bar for claiming each Ace must be defined by management through the Critical Qualifying Questions (CQQs) in the sales process and rigorously applied by your sales team. **The Critical Qualifying Questions are not optional behaviors**—they are now part of the job description requirements for continuing in sales with your firm.

Here's how the forecast math works.
Each Ace is worth twenty-five percentage points in the forecast process. If you have a pending piece of business at fifty percent, it means two qualifying Aces are completed with two remaining. This can all be reported on a summary spreadsheet and/or built into your customer relationship management (CRM) system for real time forecast updates. The following page illustrates the Four ♣ Aces forecast spreadsheet we use in our business.

Weekly Pipeline Report

Due Every Friday By 9 AM

Name:

Date:

S-P-C Status	Name	Product or Program	Contact With Emotional Dec. Maker	Motivation Fit ♣	Money Defined ♣	Methodology Accepted ♣	Market Options Eliminated ♣	Terms and Schedule Complete	Close Date	Current Points		Revenue Potential	Net Forecast
	Example Co.		X	*25*	*25*			X		*50%*	x	*$40,000*	*$20,000*
										0%	x		$0
										0%	x		$0
										0%	x		$0
										0%	x		$0
										0%	x		$0
										0%	x		$0
										0%	x		$0
										0%	x		$0
										0%	x		$0
										0%	x		$0
										0%	x		$0
										0%	x		$0
										0%	x		$0
										0%	x		$0
										0%	x		$0
										0%	x		$0
										0%	x		$0
										0%	x		$0
										0%	x		$0
										0%	x		$0
												Total	$20,000

S-P-C Status:

S = Initial Contact Made. (SUSPECT)

P = Motivation Fit. (PROSPECT)

C= Current Customer with New Business. (CUSTOMER)

A downloadable version of this spreadsheet is available on our website at www.CROsuccess.com

Chapter 17

FORECAST MIX

If you're not managing the new and repeat business arriving on your sales forecast, you may not be noticing if you're obtaining a high percentage of repeat business (farming) on the forecast. This business is valuable, but without new accounts (hunting), your business may become stagnant.

What is the percentage split between new and repeat business on your current sales forecast?

We don't have a specific new account business vs. repeat account business ratio for you to target as it's different in every industry, but we do have a lifetime of feedback from clients saying they don't have enough new accounts in their forecast.

In any company, new business is critical for future growth. If your current sales forecast is mostly repeat business, not only should you look at the sales process, but also the core profiles of your sales people. It may be that your team is loaded with Farmers and not Hunters. The most effective solution for determining the natural sales style of your sales team starts with your talent selection process (see Section V).

Chapter 18

FORECAST REVIEWS

Ideally, sales would like every prospect to say, "I must have your product today. Money is already allocated and available. I am the final decision maker and all other options have been considered and eliminated so how soon can you deliver?" (A true Four ♣ Aces forecast opportunity.)

The reality of getting to Four ♣ Aces usually requires multiple prospect events depending on your sales cycle. During the Critical Qualifying Questions part of the process, each Ace added by the rep on to his/her forecast has an audit trail back to the prospect discussion (who, when, etc.) and the answers given.

When sales management meets with a salesperson to discuss and review the rep's forecast, two **drill down** questions are asked regarding each piece of business listed:

1) Explain how you obtained the Aces claimed on the forecast. *This becomes an audit review of the Critical Qualifying Question events for each Ace claimed regarding the specific prospect.*

2) What is your plan and schedule to qualify the remaining Aces with each prospect? *Let the sales rep explain how and when he/she will either move the prospect* ***up*** *or* ***out*** *based on the Critical Qualifying Question events the sales rep has remaining to complete.*

Note: Many clients have installed both their Critical Qualifying Questions and forecast forms in their CRM software platforms. This aids compliance and can provide automated updates regarding pipeline changes. It is worth consideration, especially if you have a geographically dispersed sales staff.

Client Example

One of our manufacturing clients in the construction materials business was suffering another year of inadequate margins and inaccurate forecasts. The sales excuses were essentially that the competition had eliminated any competitive advantage and the products had truly become a commodity. On top of that was yet another overly optimistic sales forecast with ever extending close dates. The sales reps had convinced the sales manager they were doing everything possible to close business.

Once we established the Bankable Forecast Process and started holding sales people accountable for the new selling process behaviors (Critical Qualifying Questions), things began to improve. The new process exposed the forecast fluff, forcing salespeople to go out and find additional prospects, and qualify them more objectively. In just over a twelve-month period, the company went from $8 million on the forecast to over $100 million with thirty percent higher margins on business they closed, all this in their so-called "commodity" business.

Chapter 19

IMPLEMENTING THE BANKABLE FORECAST PROCESS

The Bankable Forecast Process "Four ♣ Aces" is based directly on the Critical Qualifying Questions for Motivation, Money, Methodology and Market. Sales people are tasked with delivering these qualifying questions and working through the prospects responses to objectively define their company's position in each deal.

Management is responsible for:

- Setting the bar in terms of what prospect responses are required for claiming each Ace in the forecast process.
- Auditing each Ace claimed (the forecast drill down) to maintain qualifying process accountability (based on the Critical Qualifying Questions) and forecast accuracy. The qualifying process is always about moving the prospect up (adding more Aces) or out (not a fit today) as well as removing Aces when the audit justification is light and the rep needs to go back to the prospect for additional clarification.

- Reviewing and coaching the salesperson's strategies and timing for going after the remaining Aces with each prospect opportunity.

A. **Bankable Forecast Process Installation Work Flow**

1. Develop and distribute a Four ♣ Aces forecast report format. A sample Excel Spreadsheet is available through our website at www.CROsuccess.com.
2. Define and communicate to the sales team the minimum bar of satisfactory Critical Qualifying Question responses required (reference Chapter 16) to claim each Ace (Motivation, Money, Methodology, Market).
3. Schedule regular forecast reviews to:
   a. Update what has been added or deleted from the previous forecast.
   b. Audit the validity of the Aces claimed for all entries.
   c. Review and coach the reps' plans to address the remaining Aces (qualifying events) with each prospect.
4. Monitor and hold sales reps accountable for completing their qualifying events as planned.

B. **What are the early indicators that the process is working?**

1. The forecast numbers dip down as the Critical Qualifying Questions process clarifies the reality of previously reported high probability deals. Some rep turnover can occur based on this new reality of a reduced pipeline.
2. Prospects that were "welded" to previous forecasts but never closed now disappear as reps objectively re-qualify the opportunity.
3. Sales talent is more visible based on their creative use of the Critical Qualifying Questions process to shorten sell cycles and produce results.
4. New business becomes easier to qualify and forecast.
5. Forecast numbers start to reflect the revenue potential of your Differentiating Value in the marketplace.

SECTION IV

Results-Driven Incentive Process

Chapter 20

INCENTIVE MYTHS AND LEGENDS

If you flipped to this chapter first for the secrets of incentives, know that the correct blending of incentives still only factors in as one of four core processes of our Revenue System. However, when designed correctly, a Results-Driven Incentive Process can have a profound impact on the revenue performance.

Before we begin, let's get it out in the open –

THERE'S NO SILVER BULLET FOR INCENTIVES.

That may not be what you wanted to see, but we'll walk you through the lessons we've learned over the decades that will save you years of agony about incentives.

Let's review the seven most common mistakes that most businesses make with their incentive programs.

Incentive Mistake #1

All business (new and existing accounts) earns the same incentive.

New account business is ALWAYS worth more than ongoing business with existing accounts because

1) it's more difficult business to obtain than continuing business with already established account relationships.
2) it's the only way your business will generate sustainable growth.

By paying more for new business, you train your salespeople to GROW your company instead of just taking the easy business (low-hanging fruit) that was likely coming your direction anyway. From the Chief Revenue Officer role, it is important to keep your company strong and growing; new business is the best way for you to accomplish this.

Incentive Mistake #2

Putting a cap on a salesperson's earnings.

If senior management sent out a message that they wanted and expected substantial growth in both revenues and profits in the coming year and in the same text announced a maximum cap on those revenues and profits, they'd be viewed as having no business sense.

Yet, we still hear of companies that put caps on their salespeople's earnings. Essentially, they have just put a cap on the company's earnings. Management tells the salespeople to sell, sell, sell, but by placing a ceiling on their earning potential, management discourages the salesperson from being anything greater than average. These companies also tend not to attract the best sales talent.

Sure, we've heard the justification for capping salespeople's earnings, "If we didn't put a limit on a salesperson's earnings, they might make more than the president." **Get over it! If the president has to make the most money, he/she should take on a Hunter/Rainmaker role in sales.** Then the president will at least have a more hands-on understanding of what is required to grow revenue and manage a herd of those wily, independent variables called prospects.

If your salespeople bring value and profits to your company, why shouldn't they be compensated for it? Great salespeople can be worth their weight in gold, and if you don't recognize that by paying them what they're worth, they will find someplace else that will.

Incentive Mistake #3

Not creating an incentive based on desired outcomes.

This seems so obvious, but is so easily missed by most companies. Here's an example of what we mean:

A consulting company offered only five-year consulting arrangements. They felt that by having this longer agreement, they would be more successful with their clients and more profitable. The sales people claimed that it was a hard sell and they'd sell more if the term of the agreement was shortened to three years.

Well, the salespeople got their wish. The company began offering a three-year agreement with one catch: it paid only a fraction of the standard incentive. Guess what, no salesperson ever sold the three-year program that they so desperately needed. The incentive program the company offered drove the business to where they wanted it.

Incentive Mistake #4
Not having a defined sales cycle.

We routinely visit companies that can rattle off a long list of quality control measurements for their production line, the daily efficiency ratios, declining warranty costs, and the failure rate of the newest product. Yet, when asked about the metrics used to measure their sales cycle, we're met with blank stares and stammers.

Having an understanding of how long a piece of business takes to go from an initial contact (cold call, web inquiry, etc.) to payment for goods/services delivered is critical for both business planning and incentive processes.
Installing a midyear special incentive program for "new business to close this quarter" when in actuality the sales cycle from new prospect to sold business is typically eighteen months will only confirm:

1. Management is not well connected to the business fundamentals.

2. The company will end up paying more commission this quarter for the "new business" that was already over a year into the sales pipeline process and coming in anyway. So the special incentive has no real impact on finding new, closeable business.

Incentive Mistake #5
Letting Finance design the incentive plan.

When we asked clients why they have Finance design their incentive plan, the most common response was, "To protect the company." We have never been able to figure out how sales success damages a business!

An effective plan is designed to reinforce both the critical behaviors defined in the revenue system and the desired results. For example, Finance typically does not think about new business vs. repeat business, the incentive for closing five new accounts in a quarter, or the incentive for closing the first account in a totally new market segment.

Sales people will respond to what the company wants when the incentive plan is well-defined and integrated into the business model. It's important that the incentive process supports and rewards a salesperson's measurable level of contribution.

Incentive Mistake #6
Paying incentives on *orders* versus customer *payment*.

Not that your salespeople would ever do this, but we have seen salespeople submit orders, get paid, and then quit only to have some of their last orders cancel or never happen…and they were *never* going to happen. This does not mean you can only pay incentives upon receipt of payment. It does mean your incentive plan should clarify that incentives are ***earned*** only upon timely payment of the complete transaction amount. The company practice can be to ***advance*** an incentive payment (full or partial amounts) at the time of order acceptance, shipment, or whenever you decide to recognize the performance, but this approach keeps the incentive at risk until the entire payment transaction is completed, not to mention it can save your company a significant amount of time and money on legal battles.

Incentive Mistake #7:
Assigning more sales leads to the reps that are NOT doing well to help them crack the incentive column.

There's no democracy here. There are reasons why some sales reps are struggling at sales. Sales management needs to address those performance issues and map out a get well plan for the non-performing rep. Always play your strongest players for a better chance at the new business opportunities.

CRO Success Rule #7:
Reward the strong and effective; don't subsidize the marginal performers.

A complete listing of the CRO Success Rules is located on page 124.

Chapter 21

FOUNDATIONS OF A RESULTS-DRIVEN INCENTIVE PROCESS

As Chief Revenue Officer, you're asked to make many decisions and most often you're supplied with information to help you with that decision. For example, the process of adding a new regional sales office can make you an expert in the property market, labor rates and competitor locations in a dozen possible cities before you make a final decision. However, when it comes to incentives, we see Chief Revenue Officers and other executives making incentive decisions without facts or data.

We have found that the most important item for a Chief Revenue Officer to understand is how the typical new business sales cycle works. By this we mean:

From Introduction *To Closed Sale*

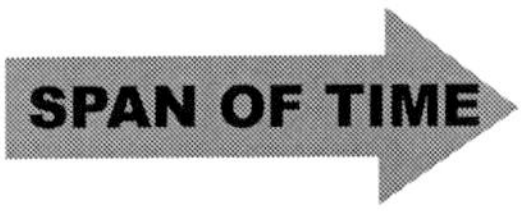

What is YOUR company's timeline for one sale?

Let's operate under certain assumptions for the sake of this example. It takes Joe Average the following to close a new sale:

> 50 prospect introductions yield 1 average sale
> A salesperson needs to close an average of 20 sales per year
> 50 introductions x 20 closed sales = 1,000 introductions

Now, some of the first things that run through a Chief Revenue Officer's mind:

- 1,000 introductions? That's going to take too long.
- We don't have that many potential clients.
- Even if we had 1,000 potential clients, how can we change the formula?
- Fire Joe.
- Hire some super rep for an obscene amount of money and get there in three months.
- Hire the competitor's salesperson. We'll get a "twofer"—the salesperson will bring business along and has already made 1,000 introductions.

There are a couple of things that are very clear in the majority of businesses: Companies don't understand the specific metrics of their sales cycle and by not understanding the sales cycle, they run the risk of:

1. Undetected poor sales performance

2. Inaccurately estimating their sales opportunities

In order to understand your sales process you must understand the sales cycle timeline:

It's important to know the specifics:

BASIC SALES CYCLE TIMELINE PHASES

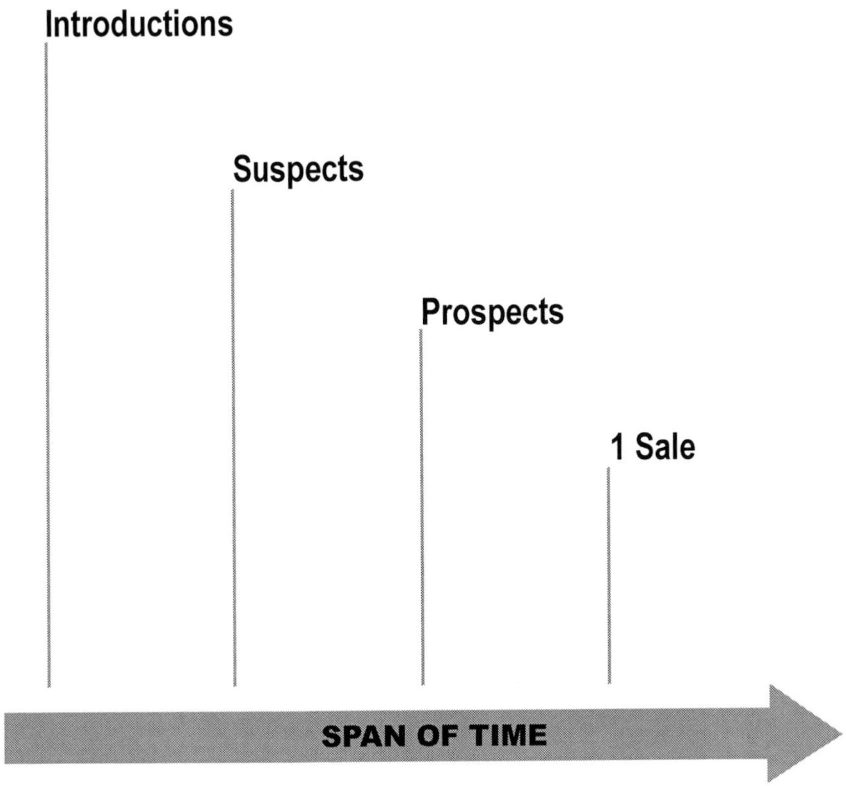

1) How many introductions do we need to obtain one sale?
2) How long is each qualifying phase of the sales cycle?

Once you have a grasp on the sales cycle timeline, you are ready to design an effective incentive program because you now know what *can* and *should* be done when it comes to bringing in business.

Chapter 22

OPTIONS AND VARIABLES

The golden rule for incentive programs is:

One size does *not* fit all!

When incentive systems are not aligned with the market opportunities and business development strategies of the company, the impact ranges from a lack of sales force motivation to ongoing turnover followed by costly recruiting, training, and account or territory rebuilding.

There is no template regarding the number of variables to consider in developing an effective incentive plan. The process can be complex, but the result must be straightforward, achievable (reference your sales cycle timeline), and focus on the role behaviors that are required to deliver the results.

After you define the sales cycle timeline, incentive plan development begins with evaluating several key areas:

- Is the business strategy based on pioneering new customers and markets or developing existing account relationships?
- What are the desired sales skills/behavior profiles for each market segment and its growth objective?
- What are the critical performance thresholds and related eco-

nomics in your business model?
- What is the industry profile regarding base compensation, commissions, bonuses, and other performance-based incentives?
- What is the mix regarding individual sales contributors and account teams?

The incentive plans we have developed to reinforce the desired outcomes typically included combinations of the following:

1) **New vs. existing business** – new accounts/markets earn more than existing renewal business. This is critical for motivating Hunter/Rainmaker talent.
2) **Threshold performance incentives** – progressive plans that pay higher incentives for higher thresholds (steps) of performance. Threshold performance incentives work better for Hunter/Rainmaker reps than straight line (one incentive for all levels of performance) plans.
3) **Consistency incentives** – performing above quota for multiple consecutive quarters, etc. This is the "treadmill" platform that helps salespeople become more strategic about reloading their prospect pipeline.
4) **Margin threshold incentives** – assumes the sales force has margin (pricing) responsibility. The bottom line here is salespeople become better negotiators when they are using their own money.
5) **Team incentives** – when the sales goals are clearly dependent on multiple participants. These plans allocate incentives by contribution including prospecting (finding the opportunity), qualifying, closing, and providing post sales support as required.

CRO Success Rule #8:
Incentives are the most underutilized tool available to Chief Revenue Officers in terms of meeting their performance objectives.

A complete listing of the CRO Success Rules is located on page 124.

Chapter 23

PAYING SALESPEOPLE

We have seen crazy pay scales over the years: overpaid account "babysitters" and incentive payouts based on the wrong elements for growing business. So we've boiled down the pay scale process to the following:

***Recognize Effort* = Base compensation**
***Reward Results* = Incentive compensation**

In *recognize effort*, we refer to compensation paid to the salesperson for executing the desired sales behaviors: sourcing introductions, making cold calls, scheduling and attending appointments, qualifying prospects (Critical Qualifying Questions), submitting accurate sales forecasts (Four ♣ Aces), providing proposals and quotes, etc., in essence, engaging in the behaviors necessary to achieve sales goals.

By *reward results*, we mean the incentive pay used to compensate those who are effectively able to translate their *efforts* into company desired *revenues*.

Okay, so you want to know the numbers. Unfortunately, industries pay differently, but pay scales still follow basic economics:

The more challenging the position, the more rewarding the results.

This applies to all organizations regardless of their size or economic condition. Start-ups and turnarounds can be extremely challenging, but we frequently see board members and investors in those situations viewing sales compensation as a necessary evil rather than a strategic investment. The "necessary evil" approach consistently produces disappointing results.

We seriously thought about including a draft of a multi-metric incentive plan, but we stopped short. We know it would be just too tempting to cut and paste the sample plan into your own sales incentive program—whether it is the right plan or not. Product margins, sales cycle timelines, growth objectives, and sales rep behavior requirements of each business are too unique to suggest a fill-in-the-blanks format for success.

We have also observed incentive plan documentation that speaks only to the commission percentages without clear definitions of other necessary terms and conditions. Below is a check list of topics we recommend for consideration in all plan documentation.

Incentive Plan Check List & Sample Terms Outline

A. **Sales Revenue**

Sales revenue is defined as the revenue for all materials/services, etc., ordered and accepted by the company based on a customer signed contract/purchase order/purchase agreement, etc. Incentive performance calculations are based on the net transaction amount after all discounts, returns, write downs, custom shipping and handling charges, etc.

B. **How Incentives are Earned**

Performance incentives are ***earned*** only when timely payment in full for the complete invoiced transaction is received. Note: The company may **advance** performance incentives based on shipments, invoices, etc., but incentives are not ***earned*** until full and complete payment is received.

C. **Dates the Plan is in Effect**

The effective dates of this plan are for orders received starting January 1, and include orders received and accepted by the company through the close of business on December 31, etc.

D. **Sales Team Splits**

When multiple sales managers/sales reps/authorized resellers are *directly* involved with orders crossing territory boundaries, branch offices, national accounts, etc., the revenue splits will be as follows:

__ % of revenue credited to the territory manager/sales person issuing the proposal/contract (this region is responsible for order accuracy).

__ % of revenue credited to the territory manager/sales person leading the negotiation.

__ % of revenue credited to the territory manager/salesperson supporting the delivery/installation/ongoing customer relationship.

E. **Resignation/Termination**

In the event of either a resignation or termination, final performance incentives will be for completed transactions (payment in full received) through the end of the previous week/month/quarter, etc.

F. **Assigned Market/Territory and Exclusions**

All forty-eight continental states excluding the states of... Territory *does not* include the following house accounts, authorized representatives, distributors, etc.

G. **Disputes**

The company reserves the right to change or cancel this plan at any time. Management's decision is final resolving all disputes.

So if we teach you anything about incentives let it be this: your incentive plan should not look like anyone else's.
That said, when creating your unique incentives, keep your sales team in mind and the types of business you currently have and/or desire. We say this because there are two basic profiles of sales-people in the market - Hunters/Rainmakers & Farmers/Account Managers and one type is far more valuable in growing a business than the other.

Farmers answer the phone.
Hunters make the phone ring

Chapter 24

HUNTERS/RAINMAKERS

The salespeople most Chief Revenue Officers want to hire are Hunters/Rainmakers. They are the ***sales entrepreneurs*** that grow business because they are naturally hardwired for only top-level performance.

Hunters/Rainmakers thrive on commission-leveraged plans where there is no cap on their earnings potential, and they make a lot of money doing what they do. Their W2 split typically ends up around one-third base and two-thirds commission.

Good Hunters are essential for growing your revenue. Keep them focused on the areas that make you the most money, incent them in those areas, pay them what they're worth and everyone will be successful.

When creating your incentive program, be careful not to structure it in a way where you actually discourage sales. Yes, this is regularly done. An example of a discouraging sales structure would be incentives based solely on the year's sales total. If a salesperson closes a large order in the first quarter, hitting the year's goal, and without quarterly incentives in place, he/she may decide to coast the remainder of the year waiting for payment.

On the flipside, if you structure incentives only on a quarterly basis, you may discourage salespeople from closing business early; instead, they pace the business so they hit their quarterly goals. This form of sandbagging is not an uncommon practice.

sand·bag *verb.* a galactic phenomenon producing a unique category of spontaneous orders having zero sell cycle time and no forecast audit trail
sand·bag·ger *noun.* a salesperson committing the act of sandbagging

Carefully balance your Hunter plans between quarterly and yearly incentive goals. Each industry's incentives will be different. A good rule of thumb is to have an annual goal that is measured quarterly with no penalties for accelerated performance.

Discount Bucket

Another incentive that we found effective for Hunters (and should *only* be offered to Hunters) is what we refer to as the **Discount Bucket**. It was developed to discourage salespeople from discounting or asking for special pricing or extra concessions in order to close a deal. We realize that sometimes special pricing may be necessary to close a deal, but how do you effectively get your salespeople away from offering special pricing on *every* deal?

There are many variations of the Discount Bucket available to generate the results you desire, but here's a simple example:

> The company offers each sales rep a discretionary annual discount account of $10,000. This money is available for sales reps to use when they feel that an opportunity needs to be pushed just a little to accelerate and secure the deal.
>
> Now here's the catch in making the sales reps carefully consider whether or not they want to dip into their Discount Bucket: At the end of the year, if the reps achieve their performance goals, whatever balance is remaining in their

> Discount Bucket becomes another incentive. All or part (typically half) can become theirs. If they used the entire bucket amount or did not make their annual goal, the additional incentive payout is zero. When the reps are giving away their own money, they become more skilled at finding ways to close the deal that do not involve concessions on price.

We designed a Hunter plan for a technology company with significant market growth potential. The individuals under the plan all performed successfully (exceeding goals, etc.), but one individual became a standout. He was fearless in terms of contacting new prospects and pushing the company's technology for specialized manufacturing applications.

The incentive plan paid quarterly (Discount Bucket annually) and was based on quarterly forecast mix—yes, forecast performance can be part of the incentive plan, actual product revenue mix, and timely customer payment performance. His revenue performance more than doubled and his Discount Bucket was *never* used (usually a bragging right with Hunters) to gain a favorable decision. He always maximized the Discount Bucket payout which required being above the 100% performance bar every year. It *can* be done.

Chapter 25

FARMERS/ACCOUNT MANAGERS

Farmers…

- Sometimes try to be Hunters, but it's usually a struggle.
- Are often found maintaining business that's already in the door.
- Tend to not do much in the way of developing new account business.
- Typically consume large amounts of the sales manager's time trying to figure out why they can't hunt.
- Will show up and interview for a Hunter position even when you are clearly advertising and seeking a Hunter profile.

Farmers can get lucky from time to time and close a deal, but not consistently. Putting your revenue generation in the hands of a Farmer is risky.

Farmers look to receive a high base (ninety percent of their W2) with the balance as commission. They tend to make considerably less than an average Hunter even when hired to fill hunting positions. And as you can guess, the Farmer never does as well at hard-core sales performance as the true Hunter.
You often will find Farmers in sales, but their sales function is more as an account manager. Maintaining current accounts is important and Farmers will do a better job in this role than Hunters.

The incentives for Farmers need to be different from their Hunter counterparts. Instead of hard sales numbers, it often makes more sense to have their incentives tied to activity milestones within their accounts.

For instance, are your Farmers maintaining regular face-time and contact with the right people in the account, mainly the decision makers? By keeping your Farmer in front of the right people and creating ways to make changing vendors uncomfortable, they will help your company maintain the home field advantage when a competitor's Hunter makes contact.

An example of what can happen if you're not rewarding the proper results for a Farmer/account manager can show up like this:

Client Story

A software company's Hunter approaches the prospect's CEO and/or other decision makers and unveils a revolutionary way to track production and sales. This software will save the company millions by reducing the time to market and administrative work. The CEO and the rest of the exec team are SOLD!

After the implementation of the software, the account gets turned over to the account sales manager or account executive, aka a Farmer. He deals directly with a lower-level IT staff supervisor and is managing the account. Periodically, a cross-sale or up-sale may happen, but this business was coming in anyway, with or without the Farmer's involvement.

Now, the Farmer and the lower-level IT supervisor speak frequently; the Farmer provides software upgrades, answers questions, and periodically takes the IT staff to lunch. Everything's going fine, right?
Well, not all things are that perfect. You see, the Farmer has never spoken to or developed any relationships with the decision makers. From the Farmer's level of interaction with the account, no one is aware that the decision makers are getting restless. In fact, the decision makers have begun taking the cost-saving software for granted and are looking for the next best thing. Now, this "well-tended" account is at-risk. While the Farmer focuses only on the lower-level IT supervisor, the competitor's Hunter is going after the decision makers about newer software solutions. Before the incumbent software company knows what's happened, they're on their way home with their software distribution kits in hand.

For Farmers, reward them in areas such as:

- Overall account growth and new projects in their accounts
- Obtaining referrals
- Success in keeping the competitors' Hunters OUT
- Building relationships with the primary decision makers

An effective way to keep competitors out is by creating what we refer to as "soft addictions." We bet that you have even succumbed to soft addictions with your vendors, for example, your bank. Banks have become masters at creating soft addictions—automatic deposits, automatic payments, bill pay, etc. These are conveniences for the customer, yet are a hassle to change when thinking about moving to a new bank.

Don't expect to have your Farmers develop the soft addictions on their own, get it set up for them. These elements don't have to be expensive, just sticky.

Section V addresses how to find & hire the RIGHT talent through the Skills-Based Staffing Process including how you discern the Farmer from the Hunter.

Chapter 26

IMPLEMENTING THE RESULTS-DRIVEN INCENTIVE PROCESS

Your job as Chief Revenue Officer is to make sure you are:

- Placing the right people in the right positions.
- Structuring their compensation plan in accordance with the skills and value they bring to the company.
- Rewarding your people based on what you need to have happen.

With that in mind, we know salespeople *always* complain about their incentive plan, but when reps own a ramping forecast, they also can see and calculate the earnings opportunity in their pipeline. If they feel the result is both achievable and rewarding for the work involved, their enthusiasm is seldom veiled in terms of casual office or team dialog. When you observe those exchanges, it confirms the incentive plan is effective. If the opposite is occurring (aggressive sales team complaints, good reps leaving, etc.), then you have a flat tire incentive process that needs repair.

Management is responsible for keeping the plan motivational. This typically requires annual updates to better align the plan with current business objectives, market conditions, etc. The changes do not have to be major overhauls, but the addition/deletion/modification of some performance categories helps keep everyone more focused on current business objectives.

A. **Results-Driven Incentive Process Installation Workflow**

1. Survey competitor plans and local industry compensation profiles to determine sales base compensation levels (pre-incentives).
2. Review budget data to determine what amounts can be allocated to sales incentives for different levels of revenue performance.
3. Determine if you need a mix of both Hunters and Farmers. Two plans may be required.
4. For Hunters, review your new business sales cycle and model what revenue ranges can be projected over a twelve month plan.
5. For Hunters, map your performance incentives (see #2 above) to revenue ranges—lower performance incentives go to the lower revenue projections, mid-range to mid-range, etc.
6. Use this data to model at least three levels of revenue performance and the corresponding incentive payouts. Assuming the payout results are competitive, these three levels become the performance thresholds for an annual incentive plan. As stated previously, threshold performance incentives are more effective than straight line (one incentive rate fits all) plans for Hunters.

7. For Farmers, incentives are based more on current customer revenue growth. Project the revenue growth ranges and allocate incentives based on the economics of the continuing business. Zero growth typically means zero incentive earnings for Farmers. These plans will include requirements to solicit referrals, maintain decision maker relationships, and monitor competitor campaigns for full incentive payout.

8. Document the plan per the guidelines in Chapter 23 and distribute.

B. **What are the early indications that the process is working?**

1. Sales reps are working hard to achieve the next incentive level threshold.

2. Some reps ask if there are higher performance thresholds with even higher payouts.

3. Competition among reps to reach higher thresholds is visibly underway.

4. Reps stop complaining while they try to figure out how to maximize their incentive payouts.

5. Lead generation (finding new leads) becomes a hot topic at every meeting.

SECTION V

Skills-Based Staffing Process

Chapter 27

IT NEVER WORKS

Often when we're called in to fix low sales, we soon realize we are not the first choice. Once the company realizes the fees they will have to pay a search firm to find and hire a proven Hunter, they decide the low-cost option is to bring in a "turbo" trainer and hope some of the sales crew will "catch fire." Basically, they rationalize that the low-cost solution is installing training on the back end—when they are already in revenue panic—and hope the non-performers who got them there will transform into super-stars. **This never works.**

One of the most interesting observations in the decades we have been evaluating, training, and growing sales forces has been the number of times when we are called in to train a sales force and discover at least a third of the sales people, when objectively evaluated, have no business being in sales. We'll just say it, they were bad hires—some could have been arrested for impersonating a sales rep! Yet, we continually see management willing to throw thousands of dollars at them for training in the hopes of getting a positive return on their hiring investment.

Note: Our clients agree that the replacement costs for a failed sales hire can easily exceed $100K based on the costs of recruiting, training, ramp up time, interim customer retention efforts, territory and relationship rebuilding, etc.

This consistent pattern of companies hiring the wrong talent led us to create a more objective selection process. The first thing you need to realize is that if you hire people who don't have the traits and characteristics (core profile) you need, you can't be disappointed when they don't produce the results you want.

If a person doesn't naturally have the Hunter instinct, no amount of training will produce a transformation. We relate it to a basketball coach believing it is possible to train height.

If a person doesn't naturally have the Hunter instinct, no amount of training will produce a transformation. We relate it to a basketball coach believing it is possible to train height. If you recruit all 5'10" basketball players, no amount of training will make them competitive against any NBA team. You can develop your salespeople to the best of their ability, but if their sales profile is limited, no amount of training will have them achieving super-star sales performance.

We've sorted through the good and bad hiring processes and have mapped out an approach for consistently finding and hiring the right sales talent in a Skills-Based Staffing Process:

1. Identify Key Behaviors & Characteristics
2. Maintain a Large Pool of Candidates
3. Screen out the Cute Puppy
4. Perform Skills-Based Interviewing
5. Present the Offer
6. Structure your On-boarding Process

CRO Success Rule #9:
Every time there is an open sales position, the next new hire needs to be at least as strong as the best sales person you currently have or have ever employed.

A complete listing of the CRO Success Rules is located on page 124.

Chapter 28

IDENTIFY KEY BEHAVIORS AND CHARACTERISTICS

We have always found that the most effective way to start is to define the sales cycle and the related sales process. This includes questions like:

- What is the primary or target market?
- Who should this salesperson call on?
- What is the market demand profile?
- How are leads generated?
- Is the market geographically concentrated or dispersed?
- What is your sales cycle timeline?

Once you have profiled the sales process, reviewed the defined sales cycle, and understand the company's desired outcomes as well as the process the Chief Revenue Officer will utilize to manage the sales force, the next step is to isolate the key behaviors a successful salesperson will need to execute *consistently* in order to perform and thrive in this business environment.

These key behaviors and characteristics are what any new sales hire must exhibit in order to be considered a serious candidate for a sales position.

As an example, consider our cinnamon sales rep (Chapter 8) delivering a time to market Differentiating Value compared to a true commodity broker selling truck loads of bulk seasonings. The two sales roles have no overlap other than cinnamon. If we want to attract serious candidates for both positions, our recruiting placements would be as follows:

Cinnamon Rep Posting

Wanted: Value Seller for Commodity Markets

We are looking for a pro that can get premium prices for real commodities.

You must be able to get in front of people who cannot imagine why they would want to talk to you and convince them that you are worth more money than any of your competitors for exactly the same thing. You understand that the opportunity to quote a price is merely an invitation to a luau where you will be the pig. If you have a track record of reaching decision makers and wouldn't be caught dead talking with procurement types, we'd like to hear from you. You will be comfortable moving across the entire prospect organization to anchor your value proposition.

We also understand you make more money than the rest of the people in commodity sales.

Commodity Broker Posting

Wanted: Commodity Rep

We are looking for an experienced high-volume commodity account manager with strong negotiation and retention skills who can maintain profit goals. You must be able to operate independently and not blink when the other side puts the price hammer on you. This is constant brinksmanship in the big leagues where you measure success by the truckload. Your customers are not particularly nice, but they pay on time.

This role clarity speaks volumes to real talent. It also reduces the number of wanna-be respondents who are not high level performers.

Chapter 29

MAINTAIN A LARGE POOL OF CANDIDATES

One of the things we learned in helping clients hire salespeople is that there is a very strong correlation between the size of the pool from which you select your qualified candidates and the strength of the hire.

Let's say you're presented three candidates by a recruiting firm (in sales, this is a typical recruiter presentation number); one is an A-level player and the other two are B players. Face it: you weren't presented with much of a choice once you nixed the two B players. If you're selecting only the best from a small pool, chances for a successful hire are not high.

We found that if you don't have at least five to ten qualified finalists from which to choose for any decent sales role, the likelihood of being able to pick an exceptional salesperson is greatly diminished. So, if your current process isn't presenting that number of qualified finalists every time you hire, something needs to change because you are selecting from an inadequate pool size.

Elements to grow the size of the qualified candidate selection pool:
First, you must be constantly in the market for candidates. Any sales force is going to have turnover in the course of the year. It's important that you quickly fill openings because sales revenue can easily erode when accounts and opportunities go uncovered and unattended.

By having an ongoing recruiting message out in the market (job posting services are readily available), you will always have a few candidates with whom you are having initial discussions, and some you may have already screened. (Screening is covered next.) That way, you'll always have two to four qualified candidates at the ready for a sales position.

Understand that the pool of qualified candidates turns over approximately every sixty days. So at any given point during the year, you'll be talking to different candidate possibilities, but you'll always have a pool of top candidates available.

When a hiring need arises, you already have an initial pool of candidates for starting the process. At this point it is very easy to ramp up the search and expand the pool of candidates, thus ensuring you have an adequate stream of applicants from which to choose.

We're seeing positions filled with very strong salespeople in less than thirty days when this technique is employed year-round. (REMEMBER: These candidates will typically be at least as good as the best of your current sales talent.)

We recently had a client who, for two years, had been looking for a high-end salesperson to operate in the central United States. This job paid a base salary of $100K, plus commission. When reaching the one hundred percent commission level, it paid in the $250K range per year. There were people on that company's sales force making $400K per year, so it was a decent mid-range sales position.

The company had a lot of trouble finding the right person. But when we revised their recruiting process and messages (adding more clarity), they started to get good hits from the right kind of talent. By clarity we mean we identified *exactly* what was expected and required from the salesperson and used that language in the ad to attract the appropriate people.

They were seeking a person who had a history of performing at a high level as opposed to a person who wanted to get to that level. By writing the ad so specifically, we were able to get the lesser candidates to eliminate themselves before applying. On the flip side, we attracted those who knew what we wanted and they were already doing it somewhere else.

In this case, when our client posted the language accurately, they had six hundred responses; one hundred people were objectively screened, and they got twelve finalists.

Two of those finalists were eliminated after the first in-person interviews. The remaining ten made it through the final interview process and eight of them were extended offers by the employer, although they were initially only looking for one.

The reason the company decided to hire all eight was because these candidates were all stronger than any salesperson currently in their eighty person sales force. The company knew there was turnover on the horizon, so they went proactive. The new people are now in place and performing according to their strengths. After six months, the new-hires were already out-performing the existing sales force.

This client now has a constant recruiting message out in target locations, focusing on their difficult-to-fill markets. The bottom line is it doesn't cost much to have a constant process that defines what you want and keeps the qualified candidate pool flowing.

Chapter 30

SCREEN OUT THE CUTE PUPPY

When you are dealing with a pool of candidates, you can save yourself a lot of time and headaches by quickly eliminating the weaker applicants and identifying the stronger talent. To do this, we recommend you screen every candidate as early as possible.

By screening, we mean you must use an objective, validated hiring assessment tool that has been specifically designed for salespeople, as opposed to any general-purpose assessment that offers a sales modification add-on.

Administer the hiring assessment screen *before* interviewing. When meeting a candidate prior to screening, we have found the human factor can sometimes override what may be a flashing red light in the hiring assessment. We refer to this as the Cute Puppy Hiring Syndrome.

The Cute Puppy Hiring Syndrome is best described by the dad who, just for fun, decides to let his kids play with the cute little puppies in a pet store. Of course, the dad has no plans to buy a puppy, this is just good clean fun for the kids. Well, a couple of puppy-breath licks and a little snuggle later, the dad turns soft and the kids walk out of the pet store smiling with their new puppy.

This happens in the workplace too. Managers may connect with an individual on a personal level and hire them based on early rapport, yet the candidate was not a good fit for the position.

In one company, the hiring manager placed a lot of weight on whether or not she had rapport with the candidate. If she had a lot of rapport, she'd then run the candidate through the screening assessment. In reviewing the screening results, she'd focus on areas where the candidate was within the acceptable range and justify around any featured shortcomings that were flagged.

The only benefit for this company was that the salespeople got along well with the hiring manager; unfortunately, the sales numbers didn't fare so well. Screening after the interview diminished the pool and skewed the hiring assessment results. This scenario missed a lot of good people. One of the things we have learned is the earlier the screen, the larger the pool of qualified candidates.

Another company with a flawed screening process was located in a more remote part of the country and claimed they couldn't find good talent in their area. This particular company had an HR department on the East Coast. The HR department did what HR departments sometimes do: they looked strictly at the resume. In this case they immediately tossed out any candidate without a four-year college degree. We know one thing for sure, a four-year degree is not an indication that a person can sell or not.

When we asked the clients if having a four-year degree was crucial for the job, they said, "No, we were just following the hiring guidelines." After showing them how to attract the right people, we suggested the company loosen up their initial resume review and then run the candidates through the screen.

As it ended up, there was plenty of talent in this region; however,

some of the really good salespeople didn't have a four-year degree. By allowing the screening process to identify strong candidates, we were able to increase the candidate pool with stronger sales talent than they had in their current sales force.
The hiring screen must objectively answer three questions:

1. Does this candidate have the skills the position requires?
2. How does the skill set align with the typical sale?
3. Does this person have any fatal weaknesses (high need for approval, etc.) for this position?

Of course, the screen should tell you in clear, simple English whether or not this person is a qualified candidate for your position. You obviously would not base your entire hiring decision on the screen; it just tells you to go ahead with the rest of your interview evaluation process. The purpose of a screen is to keep out people who aren't hard-wired for your sales position profile to consistently deliver the right behaviors for the job.

By hard-wired we simply mean that in your natural state, you are energized by doing the behaviors the job requires. For example, some people love to fish and could do it all day, every day. Others out there could take it or leave it, and in reality they find it boring. So hiring the person who isn't hard-wired to fish could be disastrous if the job required fishing all day. Yes, a lack-luster fisherman could fish for a time, but he'd probably not be very good at it and would eventually quit—especially if he actually had to live off what he caught!

By hiring a person who doesn't naturally possess the skills required for the job, you're fighting an uphill battle. As mentioned earlier, you can't train height.

Chapter 31

SKILL-BASED INTERVIEWING

Interviewing a sales candidate is challenging partly because you NEVER see a bad sales resume! Almost everyone who responds is some type of "water walker" extraordinaire in that they have personally kept an impressive list of companies on the high road to success and now they appear to want to do that for you. These candidates usually have at least enough interpersonal skill to get you comfortable with them, even if they have fatal hidden weaknesses and some flawed history. As part of the initial interview process, we recommend you get:

1. A signed release form for a complete background check. This can be done more quickly through an outside resource at very reasonable fees.
2. Copies of each candidate's previous W-2s. It is one thing to claim an impressive earning history and another thing to prove it.

You won't be the first Chief Revenue Officer to have candidates withdraw from consideration when faced with these requirements.

There shouldn't be anything warm and fuzzy about the initial interview. You need to witness first-hand how effective candidates are in establishing rapport, and observe their skills for handling some rejection and disagreement. The more you model the initial interview as a simulation of the sales calls they will need to perform, the better assessment you have of overall applicant proficiency in your sales role. Resist the temptation to take control of the interview—this is an initial test event and you want to see how the candidates conduct themselves.

All interviews typically include questions regarding past accomplishments, and the responses provided by sales candidates routinely include impressive achievements. Always ask for names (former managers, co-workers, customers, etc.) you can contact to confirm their performance.

Plan on multiple interviews with these candidates. At least one of the interviews should be in a more casual setting—a coffee break outside the company or over an informal meal. Watch how they conduct themselves in a situation where they can be a little more relaxed. You want to see how they handle challenging questions in a more comfortable setting. Next, make certain to ask questions that pull out the weakness identified in the screening assessment. A good screening assessment will highlight the areas of weakness and provide you with interview questions designed to further unveil possible concerns based on the screening results.

CRO Success Rule #10:
Candidate interviews need to be a simulation of the sale you expect them to conduct.

A complete listing of the CRO Success Rules is located on page 124.

Chapter 32

PRESENTING OFFERS

Once you have screened, interviewed, and are ready to select your candidate, there is one important topic to address: You do not want to end up in a bidding contest with the applicant's current employer or another prospective employer.

The best way to avoid the bidding contest outcome is to pre-qualify that the candidate is ready to decide as soon as you make an offer. We suggest the following type of dialog prior to putting together the offer package:

"Assuming we meet and extend an offer that includes these provisions... and satisfy your questions regarding the offer, what happens at the end of our discussion?"

You want to hear a response that clearly speaks to accepting the offer. If that is not forthcoming, this may not be your candidate for two reasons:

1. Salespeople who can't make a decision usually can't get prospects to make decisions either.
2. If the candidate is thinking about taking your offer and going shopping, this is where you'll discover it, and you can now prevent that from happening.

Again, it is absolutely critical that you pre-qualify the candidate before you put an offer on the table.

Chapter 33

STRUCTURED ON-BOARD PROCESS

One of the biggest wastes we see in any sales hiring process is the lack of a clear, consistent, on-boarding (orientation/ training) process for new salespeople. Without it, you are typically restricted to hiring only people with industry experience. There are times when industry experience is essential, but they are rare. Mostly we hear companies saying they have to hire industry experience simply because they don't have an on-boarding process.

One of the discoveries we have observed over the years is that **sales talent will trump industry experience** in about ninety days.

If you currently don't have an on-boarding process, consider an e-learning approach. Web-based learning tools are readily available, plus, doing it this way, you don't have to consume as much management time in the delivery process. This is a great way for you to make certain your people are trained, tested, certified, and ready to do the rudiments of your sale.

Here is an example of an e-learning effort: An on-boarding project for a $7-billion company took less than ninety days to complete. The information collection phase totaled six weeks of a project manager's time plus coding totaled three weeks of an e-learning expert's time. There were reviews and edits along the way that totaled another four weeks to produce an electronically deliverable on-boarding process that only needs to be supplemented with scheduled face-to-face training by the manager.

When you are designing your on-boarding process, map out the first ninety days of behaviors for your new hires so you know they get a complete ramp to hit the ground running. Add simple daily or weekly performance metrics to insure new employees are progressing satisfactorily.

Chapter 34

IMPLEMENTING THE SKILL BASED STAFFING PROCESS

Our process for finding and hiring sales talent is based on client success. Not every hire is successful, but the odds are significantly better with this more structured, objective process.

Management is responsible for avoiding the two most frequent staffing errors we see today:

1. Not eliminating marginal performers.
2. Not filling openings with better talent than the salespeople in place today.

Both are toxic moves in terms of revenue growth. Chief Revenue Officers own the hiring decision and must set a high bar for candidate selection or risk a self-inflicted revenue gap down the road. The best way for management to avoid these revenue gaps is to hold regular reviews of new hire performance and update the screening assessment profiles based on those reviews. Updating the screening profile only when you are starting a new hire activity is far less effective than maintaining an ongoing update process.

A. **Skills-Based Staffing Process Installation Workflow**
   1. Based on your sales process and sales cycle profile, identify the key behaviors and characteristics a candidate must possess for the position.
   2. Post this listing (reference Chapter 28) with recruiting services to establish a pool of candidates for future openings.
   3. Select a sales applicant screening assessment and screen several candidates at least once per quarter to identify the ones qualified for future consideration.
   4. Interview, select, and make offers (per Chapters 29 and 30) as openings develop.
   5. Define what new sales hires need to know (Differentiating Value, Critical Qualifying Questions, Four ♣ Aces Forecasting, etc.) after the first sixty to ninety days on the job and develop the appropriate orientation and training schedules.

B. **What are the early indicators that the process is working?**
   1. You have three screened and qualified candidate resumes on file at all times.
   2. Unplanned openings are filled with better talent within thirty days.

SECTION VI

The Sales Revenue System 2.0 in Motion

Chapter 35

THE CHIEF REVENUE OFFICER LEADERSHIP ROLE

The Chief Revenue Officer leadership roles of **coaching, enforcing accountability, motivating, and staffing** are aligned with each of the four interrelated Sales Revenue System 2.0 core processes as follows:

Coaching > 5 M's Sales Process

The nemesis of all selling efforts is qualifying. No sales rep, sales manager, or Chief Revenue Officer likes to get a no, but when there is no alignment between your Differentiating Value and what the prospect needs, wants, desires, can afford, etc., the outcome is predictable. In those situations, it is always better to get the decision earlier rather than later in the sales cycle, which is process clarity—not failure.

The 5 M's Sales Process behaviors require your reps to do the qualifying up front. The coaching role consists of helping your team advance their qualifying skills (and shorten the sales cycle) using the Critical Qualifying Question tools. Clients typically add Critical Qualifying Question role-plays to sales meetings for both fun and an opportunity to advance the team's skill levels by seeing how others are using the same tools in the widest variety of prospect situations.

Accountability > Bankable Forecast Process

Forecast accuracy is the accountability objective built into the Bankable Forecast Process. The Critical Qualifying Questions make forecasting an ask-and-answer-based process. Using the drill down questions to audit the quality of the Aces claimed and to review the rep's plans for addressing the remaining Aces provides the Chief Revenue Officer with both a quantitative forecast number and a quality assessment of the rep's skills and competence. The Chief Revenue Officer can remove Aces from the forecast and send the rep back to do it again as required. The bottom line is the Chief Revenue Officer either gets a good forecast number or the rep gets a do-over assignment. Either way, forecast data only improves.

Motivation > Results-Driven Incentive Process

As stated earlier:

CRO Success Rule # 8:
Incentives are the most underutilized tool available to Chief Revenue Officers in terms of meeting their performance objectives.

The good salespeople work on goal time—meaning they will work as necessary to close the deal and not ration their efforts based on 9-5 clock time. They are motivated to achieve, and incentives serve as both their personal scorecard and their reward. As such, performance-based incentive plans can open the door to additional goal time sales efforts without incremental cost to the company. The opposite situation can also happen. When incentives are not meaningful or achievable, even the good sales people will work clock time...while they search for a better opportunity.

The incentive process requires commitment and creativity by the Chief Revenue Officer to deliver an effective plan. You will know you have achieved that when the good performers ask for the same plan next year.

Staffing > Skills-Based Staffing Process

The sales staffing process is transforming today from art to science. Not that long ago, reps were hired because they had a good personality or the right background. No one kept data, but based on our experience, those candidates worked out *less than twenty percent* of the time. The other eighty percent were just referred to as bad luck hires!

The screening assessment tools available today answer the question: Can this person do the job? That does not guarantee the candidate is a fit for your company culture or business model, but it does indicate whether or not the person has the core skills and characteristics to be successful in your sales role. Once you have defined your Selling Process (5 M's), Forecasting Process (Four ♣ Aces) and have a Results-Driven Incentive Process, identifying the key behaviors and characteristics for success can now be objectively described. This objectivity is the key that enables the web-based screening and evaluation tools to identify qualified candidates. Talent is never a commodity, so Chief Revenue Officers using these screening and evaluation tools today are finding the talent while others are still gambling with the old bad luck hiring model.

Chapter 36

GOING FOR THE GOLD

The Sales Revenue System 2.0 is not an auto pilot program. The most frustrating event we witness is when a company begins to slack off and allows one or more of the four interrelated Revenue System core processes to go astray.

Think of it like this: A high performance Revenue System is similar to a high performance automobile in that four primary subsystems (electrical, cooling, fuel and suspension) need to be constantly monitored and kept tuned for best performance. If any one of these processes is out of spec, you won't have a very long or enjoyable ride.

The same is true for your Revenue System. Consistently keep your four core processes "tuned" and your Revenue System will be able to produce maximum results. This is important, so we're going to say it again: **Consistently keep your four core processes "tuned" and your Revenue System will be able to produce maximum results.**

Like the Olympics, Chief Revenue Officers go for the Gold.

Good Hunting,

Carl Moe

SUMMARY

SALES REVENUE SYSTEM 2.0

Appendix
CRO Success Rules Summary

Rule 1:
When all four tires on your car are flat, putting some air in one tire does not remedy the situation. This is why most companies feel sales training doesn't work, and it won't work as long as they ignore the other critical processes of a complete Revenue System. Page 4

Rule 2:
If you're not clear about what makes you worth more, you will *always* compete on price. Page 28

Rule 3:
If a prospect decides not to do business with your company and there is no impact in the prospect's world as a result of that decision, he/she made a good business decision. As such, your Message objective is to make sure prospects understand what they will give up (lose) if they decide not to do business with you. Page 29

Rule 4:
For a shorter sell cycle, your message(s) should be directed toward the emotional decision makers describing what they will LOSE without you. Page 33

Rule 5:
The breadth and depth of your Differentiating Value platform determines the amount of traction your product or service has in target market segments. It also determines the level of premium pricing you can achieve. **If you have zero Differentiating Value, it means you are selling only on price.** Page 35

Rule 6:
A prospect can never have too much Motivation regarding your Differentiating Value. Page 40

Rule 7:
Reward the strong and effective; don't subsidize the marginal performers. Page 78

Rule 8:
Incentives are the most underutilized tool available to Chief Revenue Officers in terms of making their performance objectives. Page 83

Rule 9:
Every time there is an open sales position, the next new hire needs to be at least as strong as the best salesperson you currently have or have ever employed. Page 100

Rule 10:
Candidate interviews need to be a simulation of the sale you expect them to conduct. Page 111

Weekly Pipeline Report

Due Every Friday By 9 AM

Name:

Date:

S-P-C Status	Name	Product or Program	Contact With Emotional Dec. Maker	Motivation Fit ♣	Money Defined ♣	Methodology Accepted ♣	Market Options Eliminated ♣	Terms and Schedule Complete	Close Date	Current Points		Revenue Potential	Net Forecast
	Example Co.		X	*25*	*25*			X		*50%*	x	*$40,000*	*$20,000*
										0%	x		$0
										0%	x		$0
										0%	x		$0
										0%	x		$0
										0%	x		$0
										0%	x		$0
										0%	x		$0
										0%	x		$0
										0%	x		$0
										0%	x		$0
										0%	x		$0
										0%	x		$0
										0%	x		$0
										0%	x		$0
										0%	x		$0
										0%	x		$0
										0%	x		$0
										0%	x		$0
										0%	x		$0
										0%	x		$0
												Total	$20,000

S-P-C Status:

S = Initial Contact Made. (SUSPECT)

P = Motivation Fit. (PROSPECT)

C= Current Customer with New Business. (CUSTOMER)

A generic version of this spreadsheet is available on our web site at www.CROsuccess.com

INDEX OF KEY TOPICS AND CONCEPTS

C.R.O. Success

www.CROsuccess.com

Minneapolis, Minnesota

C.R.O. Success is our company name and our mission. We develop and deliver the tools, processes, and systems C.R.O.'s need to succeed.

If you would like to provide feedback or comments regarding this publication, please email: Feedback@CROsuccess.com

We welcome all inquiries regarding any revenue system topic.